AVERAGELY RICH

BEVAN GANG, PhD

Evidence-Based Approach for the Average Person To Start Their Personal Finance and Investing Journey

AVERAGELY RICH

BEVAN GANG, PhD

Published by Gang Lambie & Sons Inc.

GANG LAMBIE & SONS

Published by Gang Lambie & Sons Inc.

GANG LAMBIE & SONS
GangLambieAndSons.com

First Edition
Printed in The United States.
ISBN: 978-1-0698006-0-2

AVERAGELY RICH

DEDICATION

I dedicate this book to my close friends and family, in particular to my son Bruce, who was recently born just last year. Less than a year later, I started writing *Averagely Rich* in the summer of 2025. He was the motivation for me to write down everything I have learnt over my investment journey, so that one day the lessons can be passed on to him. Hopefully it'll give him the head start that I never had, and to not make the same mistakes I made early on in my personal finance and investing journey.

DISCLAIMER

The information, ideas, and opinions presented in this book are based solely on the author's personal experiences, research, and investment journey. They are provided for general informational and educational purposes only and do not constitute financial, investment, legal, or other professional advice.

Every individual's financial situation is unique. Readers are strongly encouraged to consult with a qualified financial advisor or other professional before making any investment or financial decisions based on the content of this book.

While every effort has been made to ensure the accuracy and reliability of the information presented, the author and Gang Lambie & Sons Inc., make no representations or warranties of any kind, express or implied, about the completeness, accuracy, timeliness, or suitability of the information, and shall not be held liable for any errors, omissions, or outcomes related to its use. All information is provided "as is," with no guarantees of any kind.

Investing involves risk, and there are no guarantees of future results. You are solely responsible for your own financial decisions and actions.

ACKNOWLEDGMENTS

I'd like to acknowledge my partner, Roxanne, a fellow scientist with a PhD in immunology. She spent time to proofread the book and to look at the data presented in this book, to make sure everything made sense from an academics view. She also gave me the push I needed to really get things rolling with this book and has been extremely supportive throughout the process.

I would also like to thank my close friend and business partner, Hadlee Lambie. He helped with the cover design by taking the perfectly framed photo of me on a boat sailing across Lake Ontario, with the CN Tower in the background. This photo would become my profile picture on the back cover. In his spare time, he is a camera lens aficionado and prolific photographer, with tremendous talent in the art of photography.

PREFACE

There is so much social media content and YouTube videos out there that are trying to sell people a lifestyle where you can retire in your 30s, drinking cocktails on the beach. But, this isn't going to be reality for the vast majority of people. You either need to be born into wealth, or have gotten extremely lucky on some huge gambles of some sort.

As I mentioned, the motivation to write this book was for my son. I didn't want him one day, when he's grown up, to stumble into this "retire early lifestyle" influencer space I just mentioned, and "learn" about "finance" from these avenues. I wanted him to know the lessons I learnt along the way about personal finance, but also supported by real data and academic research, and what is realistically achievable for the average person. In writing this book, I also hope that it helps anyone else that comes across it.

Most of the famous personal finance books are from American authors. I wanted to write this book to also include an appendix at the end that is tailored towards strategies for Canadians (since my son is Canadian) - the rest of the book applies to anyone everywhere, and you can skip the appendix if you're not Canadian.

I also wanted to write this book to share the lessons from my journey of 10 years thus far, because I wanted to show that it is possible to build financial security and invest as optimized as possible that a regular person can do so. That this can be done as just average people working regular jobs, even with small amounts of starting capital, hence the title *Averagely Rich*. I also wanted to give hope to those that may be less privileged, and show them that it can be possible.

My life started far from wealth. I was born in New Zealand

to two immigrant parents and grew up in a council flat (social housing) until I was 17. I was made very early on in my childhood to be very aware of the stresses, trials, tribulations and heartaches that money struggles can bring. I hope this book will give readers that are in a non-ideal financial situation in life, some hope that there can be a way out and up.

Although having been an investor for a decade now, my journey in life didn't start off with any knowledge or awareness of finance and business. My parents came from a communist country with no knowledge of a free market, investing, or stocks. Once I left home at 18, I studied science (biology) at the University of Otago in New Zealand, eventually heading to Australia and completing my PhD in cancer cell biology at the Australian National University. My mentor was Dr. Anneke Blackburn. Anneke was a very laidback stereotypical Aussie, and made my time during my PhD one of the most exciting periods of my life - I was always excited going to bed in anticipation of the next day's experiments in the lab that could unravel a small part of biology's complexities. During this time, I read a lot of research papers, as well as old seminal research papers and books about scientists. My most memorable book would be reading *Rosalind Franklin: The Dark Lady of DNA*. Rosalind Franklin would become my hero in science.

After completing my PhD, now 25, I was pretty sure a career in science was my passion in life. During my PhD, I had attended a cancer conference in Lorne (near Melbourne, Australia). As a young scientist, I was completely captivated by the closing presentation of the conference given by Dr. Tak Mak. Tak is a legendary Canadian scientist who discovered the T-cell receptor in 1983, a major component of our immune system that detects "foreign intruders" like bacteria and viruses. The research data he presented was absolutely cutting edge and tackled some of the biggest problems in cancer - I was inspired and fascinated by how much there was still to discover about biology.

I decided I would try applying for a post-doctoral fellowship (the "training" job you have after your PhD) in his research group at the University of Toronto. I interviewed for and ended up getting an offer for a post-doctoral fellowship under his mentorship, and that is how I ended up in Canada. After the first year of my post-doctoral fellowship, true to life's unexpected twists and turns, I realized that I was way more interested in business and finance. So without a degree in finance, I decided to start my journey in personal finance and investing in my own spare time. The first year or so was mainly spent reading and learning about stocks and bonds.

As an academic and scientist by training, I wanted to write this book in a way where it was supported by data and numbers, as well as research from academic research papers (studies conducted by academics at universities, that have been published in academic research journals for peers in academia to read and review). Numbers are numbers to me, whether from the measurements of cancer cell growth vs. stock market growth, or measurements of lab experiment standard deviation vs. investment fund volatility. As such, I've managed to draw on my analytical experience from science, and take a data-driven approach to this book by reviewing data from historical stocks and bonds datasets, and academic research studies.

Finally, I also wrote this book, because a lot of the investing and personal finance books out there are hundreds of pages, full of blocks of text. I've written *Averagely Rich* to summarize the main points I make by using simple graphs and tables, to have a simple as possible visual take home message. Hopefully, the journey reading *Averagely Rich* will be enjoyable, easy to understand, and help you get started on your personal finance and investing journey.

CONTENTS

CHAPTER 1 INTRODUCTION

Personal finance and investing is something that many people may be confused about, have little knowledge on, or even fear. Managing money is not something that is really taught in schools nor something that is usually talked about growing up, or even as adults. But the reality is that starting your journey to investing and having healthier personal finances is now getting easier and easier. This book is written in a way that provides a guide and journey to personal finance that has worked for me personally, and it will be straight to the point and include data, academic research, and easy visuals (graphs and tables) with simple take home messages.

The purpose of this book is to give examples using data, on how it can be possible for average people working regular jobs, to invest and build financial security realistically (that's how I came up with the book name *Averagely Rich*). This book won't teach you how to become ultra wealthy, get rich quick, or retire by 30 sitting on the beach drinking margaritas, but it will help you build financial security. Financial security will help you weather storms in life such as job loss from mass layoffs, recessions, health issues, leaving a toxic workplace and so on, as well as help you be prepared for retirement. I believe this would be more useful than something that tries to sell a lifestyle of retirement at 30 years old, spending days on the beach, which simply isn't possible for the vast majority of people. You'd either need to already be born into wealth, or have gotten incredibly lucky with a stock pick gamble (or some other type of gamble or the lottery). In the introduction, we'll cover:

- What investing means.
- What is the stock market.
- Glimpse into the key to success.

Everyone has probably heard of investing and the stock market, but what exactly is the stock market? Well, as companies grow, they can get to the point where they are ready for and want big expansion, which means they need more money from investors. This is where companies then go public through an IPO (Initial Public Offering) on the stock market, in which they offer stock (ownership of the company i.e. equity) in individual units called shares, for the general public to buy. The IPO process thus allows the company to raise more capital from the public, who invests through buying shares. Buying shares means you become an owner of the company. A company on the stock market has shares that are priced based on the aggregate of everyone's thoughts of what it should be valued at, i.e. the market price.

Don't think of stocks as getting rich quick or chasing gambles/the next big thing, but rather, think of it as being a business owner and reaping the rewards of a company's profits. Stocks are an asset - something you own that has value, as opposed to liabilities like credit card debt. Each country will have its own stock exchanges, which is where company stocks are listed for buying and selling, and collectively, the stock exchanges make up the stock market. The most famous stock exchanges are the NYSE (New York Stock Exchange) and Nasdaq from the US, in which the biggest most well known companies have their stock listed on either of the two exchanges, including companies from Apple to Walmart.

So why bother investing in the stock market? It's one of the most historically successful ways to generate wealth. The US markets, for example, have historically grown roughly 10%

annually[1]. That means that if you invested $1000, it'll grow to $1100 in a year on average. Doesn't sound much does it? But there's compounding which will eventually make that number big, and this will be covered in the next chapter. By investing in the global markets as a whole through investment funds (basically a "basket" of many stocks, which will be discussed in Chapter 3) that track market indices from around the world, you capture the continued long-term growth of the world and humanities ingenuity and innovation. So what exactly are indices? A stock market index tracks companies in a particular sector and/or country. For example, the S&P 500[2] tracks roughly the largest 500 US companies, and the S&P/TSX 60 tracks Canada's roughly biggest 60 companies. In these indices, the more valuable the company, the more of the index it will make up, because they're market capitalization-weighted.

The market capitalization (market cap for short) reflects what the market believes a company is worth, based on the value of all its outstanding shares at a given time. Which means it is not necessarily a correct valuation, nor the actual intrinsic value of a company. The market cap is calculated by:

[Current Share Price] x [Number of Shares Outstanding]

The number of shares outstanding is the total number of shares owned by shareholders, including retail investors, institutional investors, and company insiders, but not those held by the company itself (treasury shares). It's important then to clarify here, that it's not so much the price of the stock that's

---

[1] Data will be discussed in Chapter 2 and 3.

[2] S&P stands for Standard and Poor's. It is an organization that creates and maintains stock market indices, which serve as benchmarks for global market performance. S&P 500® is a registered trademark of S&P Dow Jones Indices LLC. All work (graphs, tables, text) in this book that references any of Standard & Poor's or TSX indices is not affiliated with or endorsed by S&P Dow Jones Indices LLC or TSX Inc.

important, but rather the market cap of a company. You always hear people say, "oh the stocks so expensive it's at $500 a share now". But just because the individual share price of a company is $500, it doesn't mean it's actually more expensive or valuable per se than a company whose share price is only $250. For example, two companies can have the same market cap (i.e. market value of the company equity is the same for both companies), but Company A with 500 shares outstanding, will have half the share price of Company B that has 250 shares outstanding:

Example of Market Cap and Share Price Relationship

	Market Cap	Number of Shares Outstanding	Share Price
Company A	$10,000	40	$250
Company B	$10,000	20	$500

So as you can see, all else being equal, just because Company B has double the share price as Company A, it is not actually "more expensive", since the market cap is identical. People believe both companies equity have the same value of $10,000. The share price difference is solely because of the differing number of shares between the two companies. To quickly summarize what we've gone over so far, you've now learnt the main basic components of investing and the stock market:

- **Stock:** represents company ownership (i.e. equity). It's an *asset* because it has value.
- **Shares:** units of stock.
- **Stock price:** current market price of one share.
- **Market cap:** what the market thinks the value of a company is, in a given moment of time.

- **Index:** tracks companies in particular sectors and/or countries.

Since the indices like the US S&P 500 and Canada's S&P/TSX 60 are market cap-weighted, index funds are essentially "self cleansing". This is because the most successful, profitable companies will generally be valued higher and have a larger market cap, and thus generally make up a bigger portion of index funds. The "winners" move up in the index, and if they ever become "losers", the new "winners" move up to replace them, hence "self cleansing". By investing in globally diversified funds (which I'll discuss in Chapter 3), you basically become an owner of all the most successful companies around the world. You will financially benefit from the profits of the companies through the capital appreciation (stock price increase) as well as dividends (where established profitable "blue chip" companies pay out to investors some of their profits, usually quarterly/once every three months).

Now here, I want to bring up the Dow Jones industrial Average, which is the second oldest surviving index (oldest is the Dow Jones Transportation, specific to transportation companies) and the oldest index that is still often referenced and quoted. I wanted to bring it up, since its history is so long, in order to illustrate the long term resilience and performance of the stock market. It was conceived in 1896 and opened at 41 points (points of an index represent the overall value of all the companies in the index). By the turn of the last century, the Dow closed on January 1st 2000 at 11,497 points. This is roughly a 28,000% gain over that period.

The markets generally go up over time, as humanity is constantly innovating, inventing and creating, resulting in companies with new products and services to meet the demands of the evolving needs of society. Yet even with this phenomenal growth as indicated by this historical data, many people still end up losing money. The question is why? And we'll discuss this in the next chapter.

The Dow Jones has not been as useful for many decades now, as it only captures a sector of the US market, tracking only 30 companies. The current most well known and perhaps most important stock market index that people all around the world use to track, follow and gauge the overall markets, is the S&P 500 from the US, which I already introduced earlier. Many of the major companies you know, that provide all the products you use every day are tracked in this index: Apple, Microsoft, Facebook, Google, etc. are captured within the S&P 500. It was created in 1957 and tracks roughly the largest 500 companies in the US.

The S&P 500 is arguably *the* benchmark for the entire global market. In this introduction chapter, I just wanted to lay out the importance of the S&P 500 and how it is in a sense an indication of overall stock market performance. Because in the next chapters, we'll be discussing a lot of data representing large-cap US equities (big US companies) which is what the S&P 500 tracks, and how these data apply to real life investing scenarios.

Many people say that the stock market is a scam, a Ponzi scheme, or just useless numbers on a piece of paper or a computer screen. But stock does represent ownership in a company. Let's take a very high profile example in history to illustrate this concept. In 2022, Elon Musk decided to buy Twitter. When that happened, the shareholders were paid out in cash, based on the price Elon was paying for the company. If you were a Twitter shareholder, then you would've been paid cash, proportional to your ownership percentage of Twitter. If the stock market wasn't real, then you wouldn't have been paid cash when Elon decided to buy Twitter. The fact that shareholders were paid, shows that stock *is* indeed ownership of a company, and the stock market isn't a Ponzi scheme.

Now with the fundamental concept of the stock market covered, here's the big secret upfront, straight to the point for success in ones investment journey: invest as early as you can, in a diversified fund that tracks the global indices. That way, you're always a business owner of the biggest, most successful and most profitable companies.

What prevents most people from starting their personal finance journey or reaching financial security, usually boils down to four things in my opinion:

- "I invested in stocks but it hasn't really gone up much."
- "I invested but then the stocks went down."
- "I don't know how."
- "I don't have money."

But the reality is that you don't need to be smart or have an Einstein level IQ, you don't even need to be rich, and wealth certainly can be generated in the stock market over time. You only need three things:

1. Power of compounding.
2. Emotional patience.
3. Keeping costs to a minimum.

Points 1 and 2 will be discussed in Chapter 2, while point 3 will be discussed in Chapter 3. There are nuances in the strategy (asset allocation, risk tolerance, cost of investing) which I'll dive into in the next chapters. But in the first five or so years of someone's investing journey, the most important thing is to just start with some sort of diversified strategy, and fine tune later. Don't get stuck with analysis paralysis, the big picture is that markets go up in the long term and compounding is important. Don't spend too much time on "optimization", pondering over which strategy is the absolute best, as achieving a critical mass as early as possible is what's most important.

CHAPTER 2
COMPOUNDING AND EMOTIONAL PATIENCE

Compounding and emotional patience, are in my opinion the two most important factors in investing, even more important than intelligence. To illustrate this simply, let's take a look at one of my favourite compounding stories: would you have $1,000,000 upfront now (but that's all you'll ever get), or take a penny that doubles every day for a month? Most people would jump at the $1,000,000, it's a big number after all. But the reality is that the doubling penny would actually end up being close to $11,000,000:

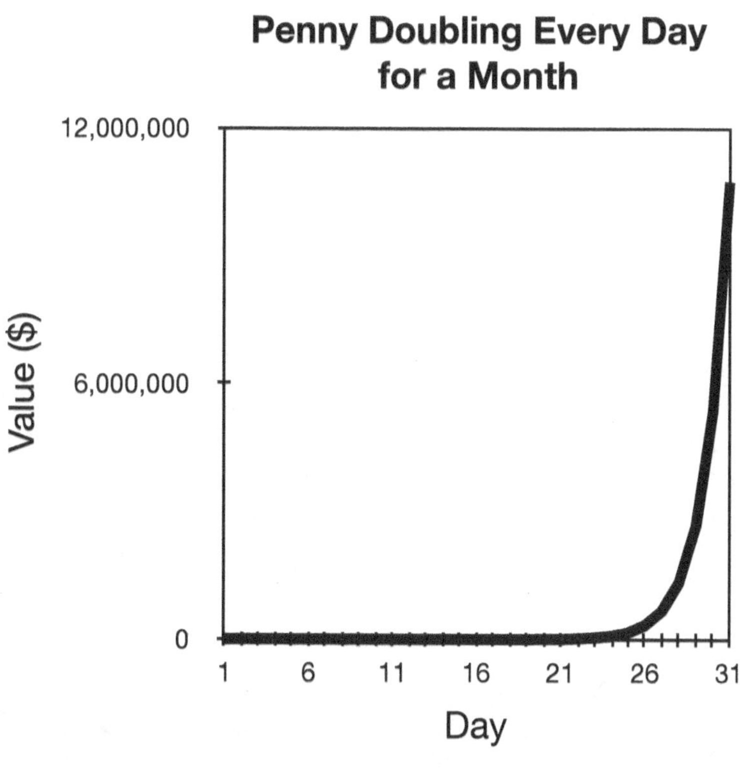

This is certainly a strong illustration of the power of compounding. But wait, there's another take home message here. Look at the numbers closely on the graph, most of the "action" in the graph happens towards the very end of the month. In fact, by day 20, you'd only have about $5,000, which is a decent amount of money and can pay for rent/mortgage, bills and groceries etc. for awhile, but hardly anything that is life changing. The next 11 days then takes this $5,000 into almost $11,000,000! This illustrates the importance of patience and compounding. You need to allow compounding to work by being patient.

So that's obviously a really extreme example, more to get my point across. Why don't we take a look at a more realistic example. So generally financial advisors say to try to save and invest 10-25% of your income. Per Stats Canada, the median salary in Canada is around $75,000 (note that this is not static and by the time you read this book, it'll likely be a different number, but the overall point I'm going to make still stands). Most people start working either right after high school if going into the trades, or sometime in their early 20s if they go to university/college for a 4 year degree.

But let's take a worse off scenario. Someone only makes $52,000, can only contribute 5% of their salary to investments, never gets a pay raise throughout their entire career, and only starts working at 25 - a much worse situation than the "average". The average stock market return is around 10% annually, so we'll use that for our projections. Even in this scenario, by the time this person retires after an "investment lifetime" of 40 years (i.e. retirement at 65), they'd have over $1,200,000, as shown in the graph that follows:

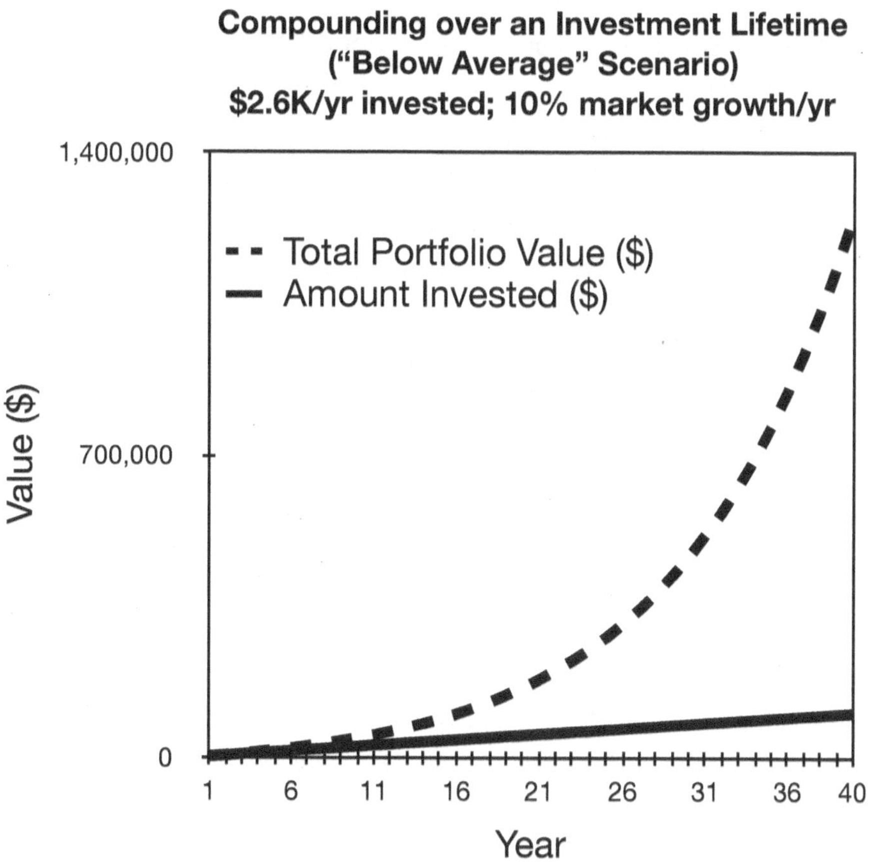

This graph also beautifully addresses one of the four main reasons I mentioned in Chapter 1 on why people don't reach financial security, and that's because they give up early, and sometimes right before when things take off:

"I invested in stocks but it hasn't really gone up much."

People invest their hard earned money, but see so little growth and they get fed up and never realize how close they were to things taking off. Take a close look at the graph, the portfolio value (dashed line) shows the total value combining both your own contributions and the markets growth over time, while the solid line shows only what you contributed to invest. The lines basically overlap until around the seventh year, in which a divergence begins to appear. The total portfolio value begins to grow exponentially and overshadows what you contributed yourself. In the end, the market growth outweighs what you can contribute from your salary, and the final amount contributed is minuscule compared to the amount from market growth.

The fact is that compounding only really begins to show up if you are consistent and give it some time. The compounding will apply to your market gains as well. For example, 10% market growth with an initial $1,000 investment in the first year brings things to $1,100. But if the same 10% market growth happens in the next year, it won't be 10% growth on the initial $1,000 anymore, but instead on the new $1,100, and so on and so forth. Compounding is therefore extremely powerful. 10% of $1,000 is only $100, but 10% of $100,000 is $10,000, which is an amount that many can only manage to invest in any given year. Here, the growth now starts to slowly outpace what one can manage to even contribute themselves to investments. There can also come a point where even if you stop investing, you'll still reach your retirement target from the organic market growth of your portfolio. This is always why it's commonly said in the investment community to do whatever you can to get to the first $100,000 as quickly as possible. In the words of the legendary late and great investor Charlie Munger:

"The first $100,000 is a bitch, but you gotta do it. I don't care what you have to do – if it means walking everywhere and not eating anything that wasn't purchased with a coupon, find a way to get your hands on $100,000. After that, you can ease off the gas a little bit."

Now we went through an example of time and compounding using a "Below Average" scenario. So let's see what happens if we use the more "Average" numbers of a $75,000 salary and investing 17.5% of your salary each year (assuming again salary never increases), with the historical 10% annual average return:

Compounding over an Investment Lifetime ("Average" Scenario) $13K/yr invested; 10% market growth/yr

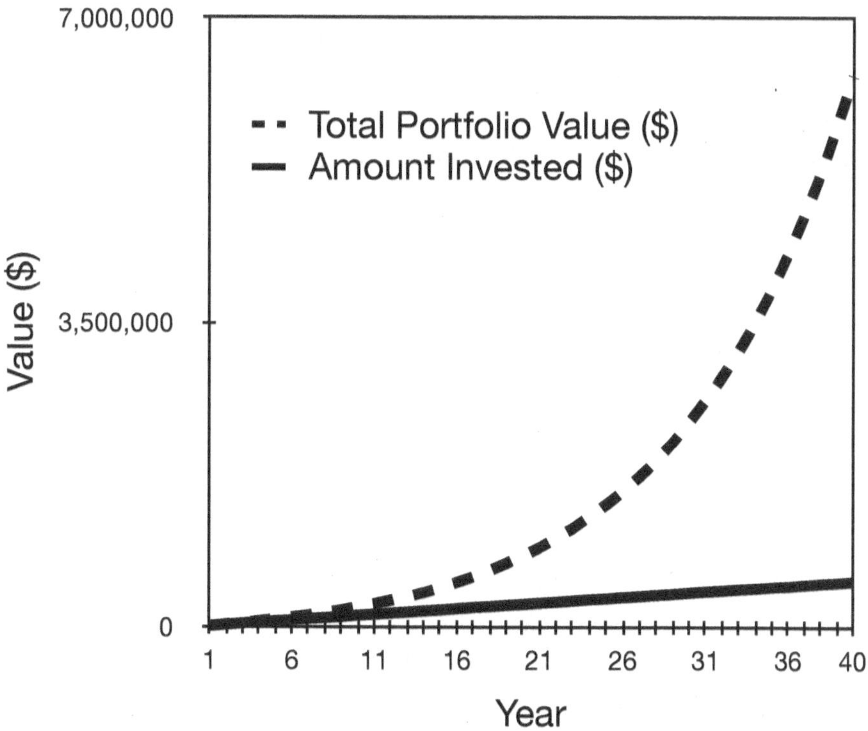

You can see now that even with an "Average" income and investment rate, one can achieve a very sizeable portfolio during an investment lifetime, over $6,000,000 by the end. Furthermore, the $100,000 mark was reached around the sixth year, in which you can see on the graph that this is the year where the total portfolio value line begins to diverge from the amount invested. In addition, it also shows you that even just six years into your journey, you can already have built up a portfolio of a size that brings you financial security. $100,000 is not completely life changing retire early money, but it certainly will help in the event of layoffs, recessions, health issues, the need to leave a toxic workplace or manager, and so on. But the main point here is both the "Below Average" and "Average" graphs, is to really illustrate the power of compounding and what could be achieved even in average households, or households that aren't as well off and below median income. What's needed really is the emotional control to be consistent through time, and allow compounding to run its course. Especially in todays world of investing where it is extremely accessible, even for low income individuals (which will be discussed in Chapter 3), something that was a drastic shift starting around 2020, in particular in the Canadian investing industry.

The final point in regard to compounding and time, is illustrating the importance through different starting ages and total final investment contribution amounts. In this example, there will be three people with three different situations, but all retiring at age 65, and assuming the historical 10% annual average return of the markets:

1. **Starting at age 25:** investing $5,000 a year, for a combined total of $205,000.
2. **Starting at age 35:** investing $10,000 a year, for a combined total of $310,000.
3. **Starting at age 45:** investing $20,000 a year, for a combined total of $420,000.

Now in this example, the second and third person start later, but attempt to make up for this by substantially increasing their yearly investment amount, which not only catches up, but far exceeds the final total amount invested by the first person that started at age 25. Now what do you think will happen? Will the people that started later end up significantly wealthier, since they invested way more of their own money? Well, let's see in the graph that follows:

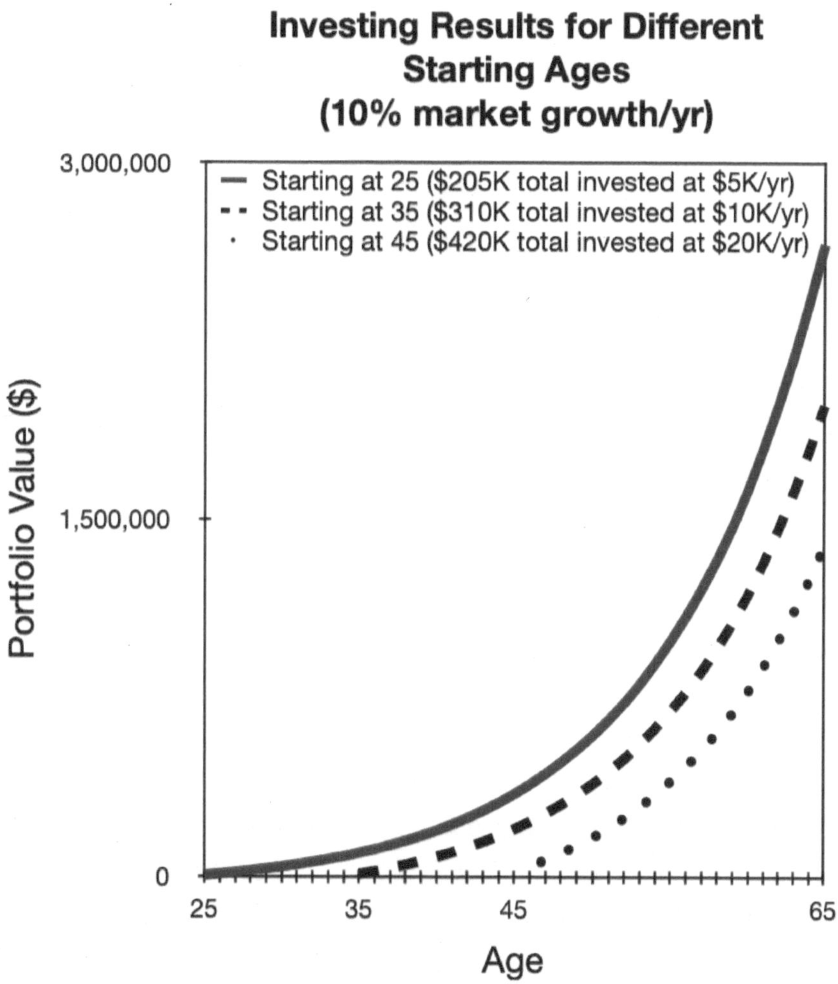

So you may be surprised that the first person that started at 25, but invested the smallest total amount, actually came out way ahead in the end. The final results show that time is one of the most important components of investing. The person that started at 25 invested less, but actually came out significantly ahead, because they had time on their side for more compounding. Now, you can't change what you already did or didn't do in the past, but here's the best advice I can give you if you haven't started yet: the best time to start investing was when you were 18-25, the second best time is today.

Now that I've gone over compounding and illustrated the overall concept with many examples visually, I wanted to move to the next important pillar of investing: emotional patience. Hopefully by this time, you've come to appreciate, based on the data from the hypothetical situations above, how simple investing really is, at least from a technical and mathematical perspective.

But as I mentioned in my opening chapter, despite the phenomenal performance of the Dow Jones Industrial index since it's inception dating back to the 1800s, a testimony to the strength of the markets over time, many still lose money investing. How is this possible?

Perhaps it is not intelligence, IQ, or education that is responsible for most of the success in investing. In the world of investing, you need to have the stomach for it. You need to be able to handle the ups and downs of the markets and the economy. This is what I believe truly separates the big boys league from the little guys that remain in the minor leagues.

While the US stock market for example has roughly gone up by 10% on average every year, it's not a straight line going up at a steady rate, as shown by the following graph[3], which shows how a $1 investment would have grown, based on the real historical US stock market performance, dating back to 1927:

You can see from the graph above, that indeed there's many periods of ups and downs. It's hard to visualize the pre-1980s data, since the same % fluctuations of the much larger absolute values in recent years, "squishes" the earlier

[3] The graphs (linear and log) have been produced by the author to show growth of $1, using annual return data calculated by the author, using raw data from the Shiller dataset, which tracks the performance of the roughly largest 500 companies in the US since 1927, and serves as a proxy for overall US stock market performance. It is found in the public domain from the open source DataHub, which has explicitly released the data under the ODC Public Domain Dedication and License (PDDL).

timepoints.

I've gone ahead and re-plotted the same data, but switching the Y-axis of Value ($) to a logarithmic scale, instead of being linear. This allows for better visualization of the earlier years of the US stock market. As you can see much more clearly now from the following graph, that there have been big up and down fluctuations throughout the entire history of the US stock market:

While the overall trend is indeed a general increase in the overall US stock market over time, it's not smooth and does involve corrections and recessions throughout its history. If we look at the actual numbers for the annual returns in the graph that follows, we do indeed see some years where the percentage drops can be quite big[4]:

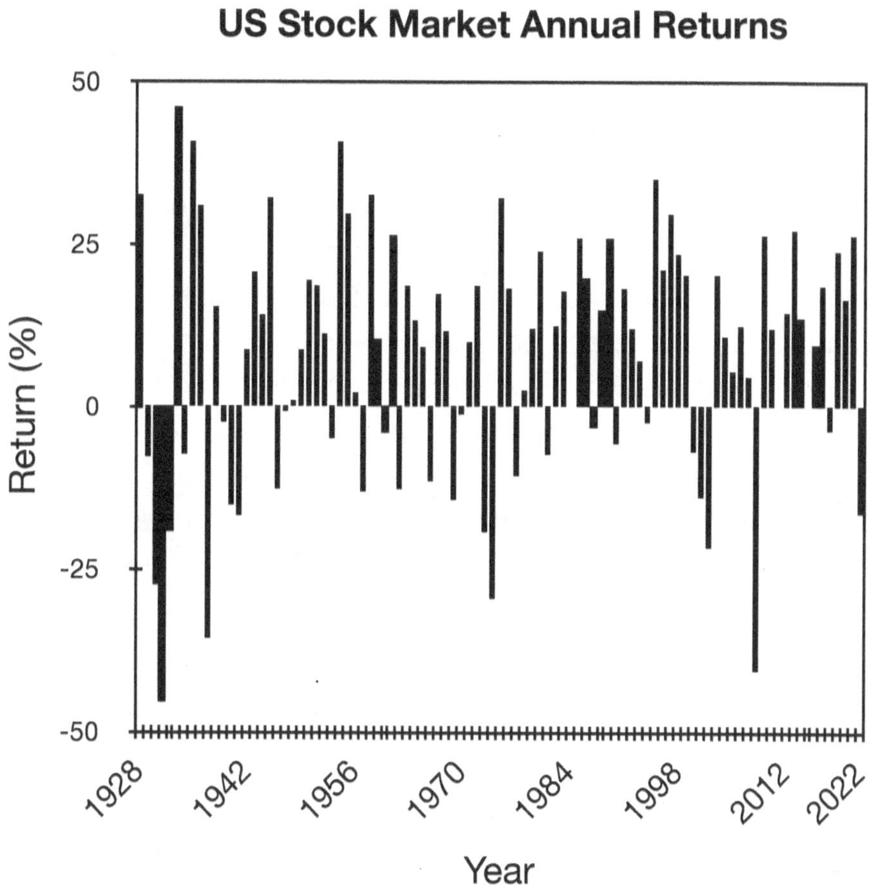

The big drop during the 1929 Great Depression, and the 2008 Global Financial Crisis, demonstrate how significant indeed that recessions can be and their impact on the stock market, which can drop by over 40% in a single year. This is essentially how many people lose money investing, despite the stock market overall returning roughly 10% a year over the

[4] The graph has been produced by the author, using annual returns data calculated by the author, using raw data from the Shiller dataset that serves as a proxy of overall US stock market performance, found in the the public domain from the open source DataHub, which has explicitly released the data under the ODC Public Domain Dedication and License (PDDL).

long term. People get spooked and panic during these moments such as recessions and market corrections. They see their portfolios go down, then begin to panic, and then they sell their investments since they worry that it'll keep going down. They've now realized a loss by doing so (they sold at a price below which they originally bought at). When the market begins to recover, they are still worried and may think it's just a temporary recovery and things will continue to get worse in the long term, so they still sit on the sidelines. Only when the market has recovered and even exceeded the previous market peak level, do they invest their money again.

By selling during the downturn, they locked in and realized a loss of their money. Now with a smaller amount of money, they use it to buy stocks later at an even higher price than they originally bought at once the recovery is fully underway. They **bought high and sold low.** This is probably the biggest lesson many investors will learn, and pretty early on in their journey. The result is they've lost money and also have an overall lower amount of ownership of companies even though they eventually bought back in.

It's important for you to understand that businesses, the economy, and the world as a whole has its ups and downs, and these impact business sales and performance, and thus the stock market. You need to remain calm and always stay invested for the long term. **Time in the market beats trying to time the market.** Now, if we look closer at the graphs though, as I already mentioned, in the log-scale graph of $1 invested in the US stock market, it's essentially always trending up over the long term, and for the Annual Returns graph, there are more up years than down years. But let's go further than just looking at the trends on a graph and dig into some actual research data and see what more they tell us.

An analysis from Cresmont Research in 2024 showed that there was no 20-year period in the history of the S&P 500 that had a negative return[5]. The analysis involved looking at the performance of rolling 20-year periods from historical data from 1919-2024. They started the rolling 20-year periods looking at the first 20 years from 1919[6] to 1938, then 1920 to 1939, and so on, until the last possible starting year (2005) that could result in a 20-year period. If you were a long-term investor, you shouldn't have lost money. In addition, the majority of the 20-year periods had substantial returns, with:

- 98% of these 20-year periods having an annualized[7] total return[8] of >5%.
- >80% of these 20-year periods having an annualized total return of at least 7.1%, going all the way up to 17.1% annualized total return.

As long as you had a long-term horizon, you would've done fine even if you had started investing during the Great Depression or the Dot-com bubble crash. The markets are resilient, and have survived through more than you probably knew. The oldest stock exchange is the Amsterdam exchange founded in 1602, the largest stock exchange the NYSE was founded in 1792. The stock market as a whole has been around for a very long time, and has survived through WW1, WW2, two atomic bombs, Chinese civil war, Korean war, Vietnam war, Middle East conflicts, 9/11, and the COVID pandemic.

Always remember that by investing in the stock market,

---

[5] Cresmont Research. "20-Year Rolling Stock Market Return." 2024. https://www.crestmontresearch.com/docs/Stock-20-Yr-Returns.pdf

[6] Although the S&P 500 was officially formed in 1957, it had existed prior as a composite index in a slightly different form (roughly 90 companies).

[7] Annualized return is the average yearly return, accounting for compounding (i.e. CAGR/Compound Annual Growth Rate).

[8] Total return means returns including dividends reinvested.

you are just being a business owner. Now extrapolate that to other ways to be a business owner to get you in the right frame of mind to think about this: if you owned a farm, would you constantly be trying to get daily quotes on its price and then panic sell whenever the price drops a bit and thus realize a loss? No, you'd hold the farm long term, wait for the harvest and profit from it.

To illustrate how detrimental trying to time the market or panic selling is, let's look at what happens if you miss just a few of the best days in the stock market. The biggest gains in the stock market actually come from a very few number of days. If we look at the growth of $10,000 invested into the US stock market over a decade (2005 to 2015), missing just the 10 best days in the market roughly halves your final portfolio value[9]:

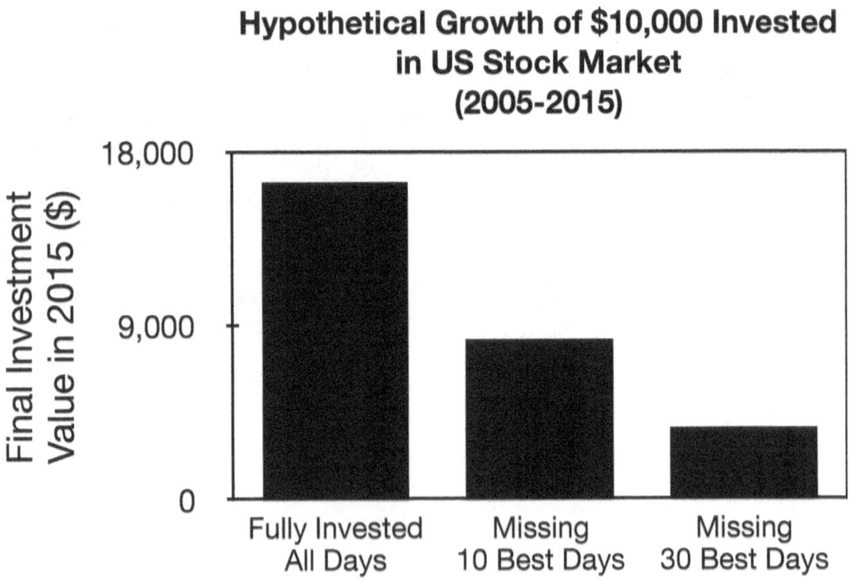

[9] The graph of the growth of $10,000, has been produced by the author, using returns data calculated by the author, using raw data from a dataset tracking the roughly largest 500 companies in the US which serves as a proxy of overall US stock market performance. It is found in the public domain from Data4Ecology, released under the Creative Commons CC0 1.0 Universal Public Domain Dedication.

Trying to time the market and/or panic selling can be very costly, as you can see from the previous graph. I wanted to finish off this chapter with a real story that solidifies what I've discussed thus far. Peter Lynch, one of my favourite investors, used to run the Magellan Fund from 1977 to 1990. It's one of the most successful actively managed funds of all time, and one of the very few actively managed funds that succeeded. The fund returned 29% a year on average, far beating the general market during that period. However, according to Fidelity (the fund provider that owned the Magellan Fund) the average investor in the fund actually lost money during that period[10]. They bought in when the fund was doing well, only to panic sell during years when the market went down (where the Magellan Fund also went down). You really do need to have emotional patience and the stomach. In the world of investing, you've got to have guts, you've got to have the stomach for this kinda stuff, this is what separates the big boys league from the little guys in the minor leagues.

---

[10] Dash, J. "How Investors Are Costing Themselves Money." Forbes, 2021. https://www.forbes.com/councils/forbesfinancecouncil/2021/06/02/how-investors-are-costing-themselves-money/

CHAPTER 3
HOW TO START

So how do you even go ahead and buy stocks to invest in companies? In this chapter, we'll go over the logistics, as well as strategy. Specifically, we'll discuss:

1. **Brokerages.**
2. **Strategy:**
    - Asset allocation and risk tolerance.
    - Costs.
    - Picking individual stocks.
3. **Retirement.**

1: Brokerages

So the biggest question many people who have not started investing yet have, will be how do I even do it? Where do I buy stocks? You need to have a brokerage account with a stock brokerage, which is a company that facilitates the buying and selling of shares for you. You don't personally visit a company, for example Reddit, and ask to buy its shares. You work through the stock brokerage. All the major banks will have online brokerage services, and in Canada for example, the Big 5 banks (BMO, CIBC, RBC, Scotia, TD) all have their own brokerage service. The convenience here is that you can easily pick the broker that you already bank with, and it allows for the most seamless transfer of money from your regular chequing account to your brokerage account, and invest from the same phone app, if both your banking and investing are with the same bank. But this is not required, and many people also don't do this. You can nowadays easily transfer money from your chequing account to any external brokerage account.

There are also popular big online discount brokerages not linked with banks, that offer services for a much lower cost, or in some cases even basically for free. In Canada for example, these major online discount brokerages such as Wealthsimple and Questrade[11] are also protected by the Canadian Investor Protection Fund (CIPF), just as the Big 5 brokerages are. Since 2020, there has been a huge shift (for the better) in the brokerage landscape. It is now easier than ever to start, as well as a much lower financial barrier to entry, and this has been made possible in part by Wealthsimple and Questrade. Regardless of which brokerage you choose (banks vs. discount brokerage), everything can now be done online and even on the banking/brokerage apps on your phone.

Today, there are brokerages that offer commission-free trading, meaning that they don't charge fees anymore for buying and selling stocks or funds (baskets of stocks). This is a huge game changer, because in the past there were very expensive fees to buy shares and thus presented a barrier to entry for many people. In addition, many of the commission-free brokerages also offer fractional-trading. This means that if you don't have money to buy a certain stock or fund because the share price is higher than the money you have available for investing, you can still invest in the company, by buying a fraction of a share. For example, if Reddit stock is trading at $300 a share, and you only have $150, you can still invest $150 into Reddit and receive half a share.

This new paradigm shift in commission-free fractional trading brokerages, means you can now invest every month,

---

[11] I am not sponsored by any brokerage, bank or fund provider I mention in the book. Any reference to any companies are not an endorsement and I am merely using these companies as examples to illustrate points made.

even if you can only spare a few dollars. The barrier to investing has never been lower. Commission-free fractional-trading is not specific to Canada, and the barrier is getting lower around the world. For example in the US, there are brokerages that offer commission-free fractional-trading as well (and probably many more than in Canada). With where the brokerage landscape is now, this essentially addresses one of the four main points I listed in Chapter 1 that prevents people from starting their investment journey:

"I don't have money."

Even if you only have $100 left over at the end of the month after paying all your necessities, and you can only bring yourself to taking $5 from that to invest, today you can! You can buy shares even if you only have $1 today, thanks to commission-free fractional-trading.

With a brokerage account setup, you can then invest in individual stocks or funds. These are identified by ticker symbols, for example the company Reddit has the ticker symbol RDDT, and you'd search for that symbol on the ordering page of your brokerage app/website, in order to purchase Reddit stock. Many brokerages actually allow you to just search for the company name, without needing to know the ticker symbols off the top of your head. You can also invest in funds, and in particular, index funds, such as S&P 500 funds which I've discussed previously. Index fund investing is generally recommended for the average investor, for reasons I mentioned in the previous chapters, primarily because you get to own the biggest and most successful companies by owning one or a few baskets (the funds).

To do this, you don't actually go to Standard & Poor's head office and ask to invest in their indices. What you do is you buy funds offered by fund providers, and these funds track the indices. The funds essentially have a ticker symbol and you put in the order to buy or sell share units of the funds, just like you would a stock of a single company. For example, Vanguard, one of the biggest fund providers in the world, has a fund with the ticker symbol VOO, which tracks the S&P 500 and is currently as of 2025 one of the largest[12] (and perhaps most well-known) fund in the world. In addition, they have a Canadian version, traded in Canadian dollars, on the Canadian TSX stock exchange, with the ticker symbol VFV, which is one of the most popular funds amongst Canadian investors. You essentially get to invest in the top 500 companies of the US and it's so accessible nowadays. It's worth noting here that if you buy versions of funds traded in a foreign currency, brokerages in general will charge you a currency conversion fee. So it's important to try to choose the one that trades in your currency and listed on the stock exchange in your country.

So essentially with these index funds, the fund providers basically do the job for you to track indices like the S&P 500, but of course in the world of business, there's no free lunch. Every fund, whether it's from Vanguard or a local bank, will have fees. We'll talk more about fees towards the end of Chapter 3, and the impact it has on your long-term investment journey.

There are two types of funds: ETFs (Exchange Traded Funds) and mutual funds. Both types of funds serve to hold many underlying assets in them (so a basket of stocks basically). The only difference is that ETFs trade like stocks, where during market hours (e.g. 9:30AM to 4:00PM EST in North America), the price is fluctuating in real time, as the fund is being traded in real time, just like a stock. Mutual funds on the other hand, don't fluctuate in terms of price during market

[12] Johnson, Steve. "Vanguard Triumphs over State Street to Take Largest ETF Crown." Financial Times, 2025. https://www.ft.com/content/641e9fd7-c989-4831-917b-23b3250be7db

hours, and instead, the price of the fund is settled after the market has closed, and that is the price you would be buying or selling at, even though you put in your order during market hours.

You may also be able to open retirement-focused brokerage account types that offer tax-sheltered growth. These are country-specific, so I can't cover every single country in this book, but you should look into these for your own specific country. These account types are powerful tools for investing for retirement. For the Canadian readers, this will be covered in Appendix 1.

2: Strategy

As I mentioned in Chapter 1, stocks are an asset as they have value - they can make you money as well. Whereas something like credit card debt is a liability (because you owe someone else money). The first bit of advice is to not start investing unless you've paid off all your debt. By debt, I don't mean something like your mortgage, or a low interest rate student loan or any other low interest debt. I'm talking about high interest rate debt, things that are roughly over 6% interest, for example credit card debt. Pay these off first, since paying off credit card debt with 20% interest means you have an immediate guaranteed 20% "return", which is definitely not guaranteed in the stock market and is far above the historical average annual return as well. In such cases, paying down high interest debt would be the most ideal choice.

Second important bit of advice for after high interest debt is paid off, is to save an emergency fund. According to the Canadian government[13] (and generally the advice that's usually given), is to have saved 3-6 months of your expenses.

[13] https://www.canada.ca/en/financial-consumer-agency/services/savings-investments/setting-up-emergency-funds.html

The exact amount is up to you and it's a personal finance decision based on what you're comfortable with.

Unless you have these two basics covered first, you're almost digging yourself into a deeper hole financially, if you choose to start investing without a solid financial foundation. You need controlled debt and preparedness for emergencies - life has many curveballs.

Asset Allocation and Risk Tolerance

Now with debts and the emergency fund out of the way, we will discuss the first part of strategy: asset allocation and risk tolerance - the two are closely related. This is essentially the step in which you need to decide where to put your money to invest, and how risky these areas are. There are two important factors to consider when deciding where to invest in and how much risk to take, and they are asset class and geography. We'll first discuss asset classes, and then move on to geography. As we already learnt, stocks are an asset. But there are other types of assets too. In terms of asset classes, the most common ones that most people will come across in their everyday life would be:

- Cash.
- Fixed income (bonds).
- Equities (stocks).
- Real estate.
- Commodities (e.g. gold, silver).

So I won't be discussing real estate or commodities in this book, and the focus will be on the first three assets. For cash, there's not much to discuss and it's really coming down to having an amount that makes you feel most comfortable, in order to be prepared for emergencies i.e. the emergency fund I covered above. In addition, to put aside cash for any near-term savings goal you have personally, such as a down payment you will need in the next few years. Again, this is very personal and the priority and how much to put aside for a savings goal is only something you can decide. For these types of goals though, you can put this money into a non-volatile investment, such as a high-yield savings account, or something like a term deposit/GIC.

For stocks, I've already introduced and discussed them, and provided the basic fundamentals, which lays the groundwork for the rest of this chapter. Now bonds are something I haven't touched on at all. But conceptually it's probably a lot easier for people to understand. Think of it as a loan. When you buy a bond, you're basically lending money to someone, they need to pay it back within a certain time, and as such you get paid interest for that period until the original loan amount is paid back. Same concept as banks charging you interest when you borrow money from them until you pay them back.

The reason why bonds are considered much less risky than stocks, and considered one of the safest investments one can make, is because when people talk about investing in bonds, they're usually referring to government bonds. For example, US treasuries and Canadian government bonds are literally the safest investments possible, as they are backed by the full faith and credit of either the US or Canadian governments. In the entire modern history of the two countries, companies have come and gone, but the countries have been there throughout. There would have to be a very severe event for bonds to no longer be a safe investment. In addition, unlike stocks, the cash flow for standard government bonds is known upfront. You know how much you're getting, because the duration of the bond is known since they come with a maturity date (the end date of the "loan"), and the interest is determined upfront (i.e. the coupon rate).

Now we've covered what bonds are as well, so now the question is, how do we strategize how to allocate our money? Do we invest in both stocks or bonds? How much of each? Well, we'd need to look at risk versus reward first. You've probably already guessed, or heard before, that stocks perform well over the long term. And indeed, stocks generally have a higher expected rate of return than bonds. Buying a stock means being an owner of a company and you reap the rewards from growth and profits. On the other hand, buying a bond means lending money only, so you just receive interest, but no share in company profits. If we look at the data, stocks do outperform bonds over the long term, with stocks growing around 10% a year, while bonds around 4%[14]. This difference is called the equity risk premium. Stocks provide greater reward, but with higher risk. While bonds provide less reward, but with lower risk.

So in general, over the long term, stocks are expected to make you more money. So why on earth would anyone want to invest in bonds, something that's expected to make you less money? As I described in Chapter 2, the stock market is volatile and I included the data to show the ups and downs of the US stock market over the last century, despite it's average 10% growth each year.

So it's certainly not a smooth ride especially in the short term. Bonds however, as mentioned, are a *fixed* income asset. In addition, usually they are inversely correlated with stocks during market downturns, meaning that if stocks do bad, bonds usually perform better. Bonds act essentially to smooth out the ride, if you were to include them as part of your complete portfolio (i.e. to include some bonds along with your stock

---

[14] Safe Withdrawal Rate. "Historical Bond Market Performance (1920-2023)." 2023. https://safewrate.com/historical-bond-market-performance.

investments).

The period of 2000-2020[15] shows how the two asset classes can be inversely correlated, as well as how over the long-term (in this case two decades) stocks usually outperform bonds:

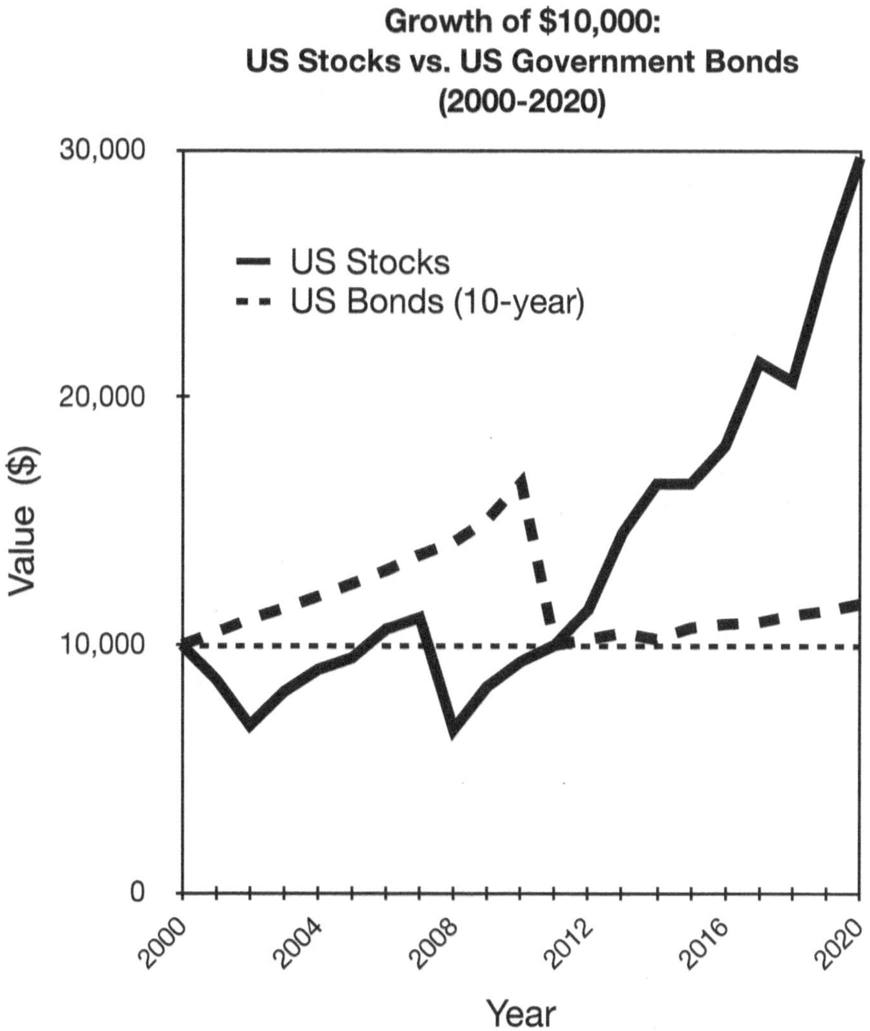

[15] The graph has been produced by the author, using annual return data calculated by the author, using raw data from the Shiller dataset that serves as a proxy of overall US stock market performance, and a dataset of US bonds, both found in the public domain from the open source DataHub, which has explicitly released the data under the ODC Public Domain Dedication and License (PDDL).

It's worth noting that while usually stocks and bonds are inversely correlated during market downturns, allowing bonds to smooth the ride, this is not always the case. For example, in 2022, when the stock market went through a correction, bonds also went down in value. This is because while the stock market was going down, central banks raised interest rates. Now just like stocks, there is also the bond market where people trade (buy and sell) bonds - the bond market is actually bigger than the stock market.

So for example, if a 5% bond was originally valued at $1000, and now the central bank has raised interest rates to 10%, why would someone pay the $1000 for your bond, when someone else is selling a 10% bond also at $1000? So in this case, the only way you'd be able to sell the 5% bond would be to sell at a lower price.

This scenario then, is what caused bonds to go down simultaneously with stocks in 2022. But in the big scheme of things, we can't really account for all the future "what ifs" moments, we just don't know, and all we can do is look at the big picture of what the historical data shows us, and that is it's an extremely rare occurrence.

Data from almost a century's worth of data shows that only in 5 years (so only roughly 5% of the time) have bonds (US 10-year treasuries) dropped at the same time as US stocks[16]. These years are 1929, 1939, 1953, 1957, and 2022 (indicated by arrowed lines in the graph that follows):

[16] The graph has been produced by the author, using annual return data calculated by the author using raw data from the Shiller dataset that serves as a proxy for overall US stock market performance, and a dataset of US bonds, both found in the public domain from the open source DataHub, which has explicitly released the data under the ODC Public Domain Dedication and License (PDDL).

Annual Return of US Stocks vs. US Bonds (1928-2022)

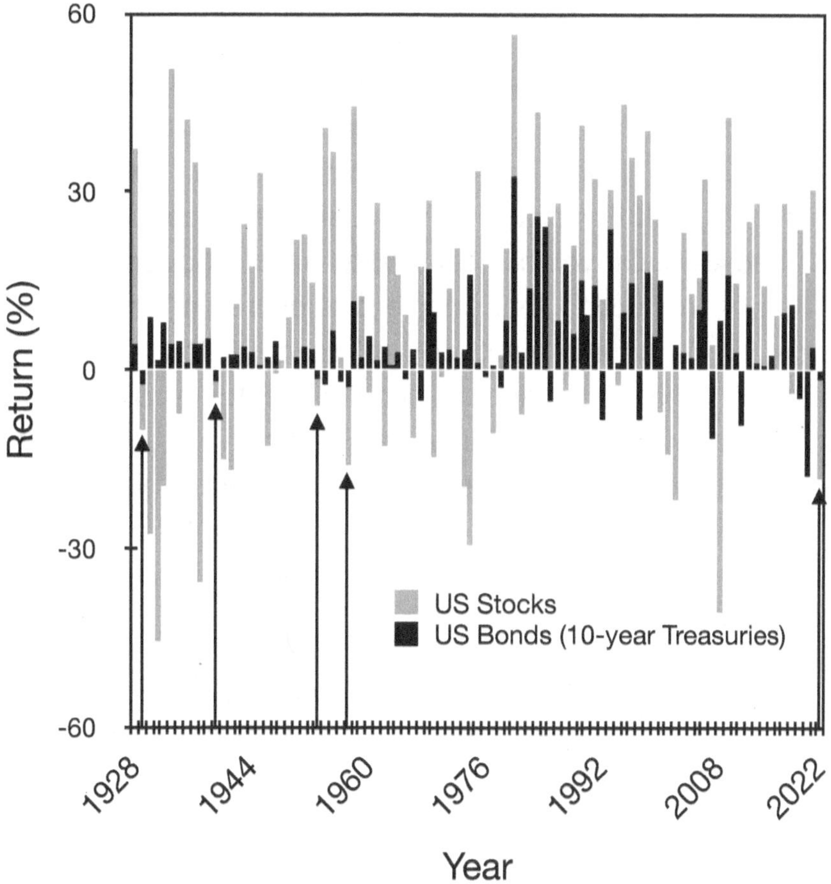

In general, bonds and stocks are inversely correlated during market downturns, and the purpose of bonds is therefore to smooth out the ride for long term investors. In Chapter 2, I also described how people lose money by panic selling, using the S&P 500 and Peter Lynch's Magellan Fund as examples, where despite the two going up in the long-term, people panic sold during short term volatility and realized losses. So bonds can play a significant role in investor behaviour and those with less risk tolerance might want to include more bonds. Not everyone can stomach the volatility of a 100% stocks portfolio. So how much bonds? Could you be someone that needs 0%, or perhaps 20% or even more at 40%?

Well, in the end, it comes down to how much volatility you can tolerate. It'll be impossible for me to decide this for you, but there are tools online. Fund providers do have risk assessment questionnaires, which help you decide on how much bonds you might need. For example, Vanguard has a popular one on their website[17]. Or, you could talk to a financial advisor.

It is worth noting that people can overestimate their risk tolerance. It appears that risk tolerance follows a normal distribution, meaning that most people fit in the middle of a bell curve, and few are in the tail ends of the curve (i.e. extremely low or extremely high risk tolerance). The graph that follows provides an illustrative example of what I mean by a bell curve and how most people fit in the "middle" (average risk tolerance):

Example of Normal Distribution Bell Curve (illustrative purpose only - data is hypothetical)

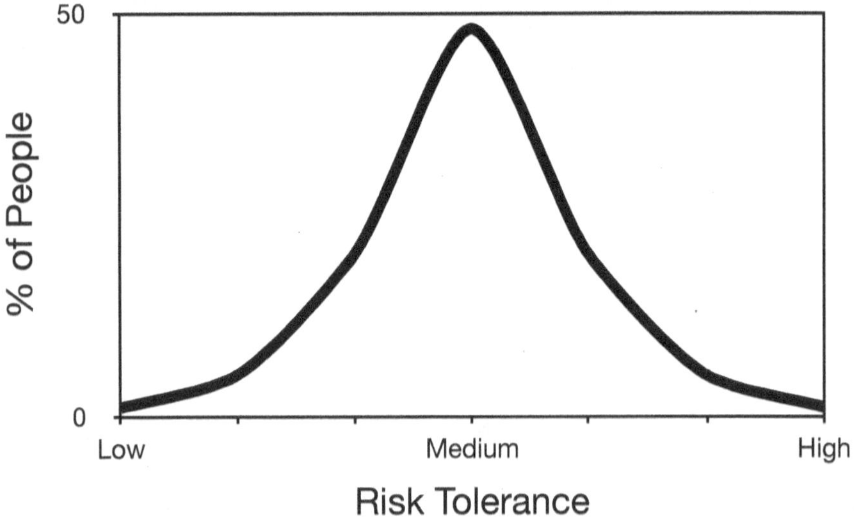

[17] https://investor.vanguard.com/tools-calculators/investor-questionnaire

Data from a Morningstar analysis of psychometric questionnaires over a 20 year period, with over a million participants, with repeat assessment before and after major crashes (e.g. 2008 and 2020 COVID) to ensure an accurate assessment of someones true risk tolerance, showed that risk tolerance indeed seems to follow roughly a normal distribution[18]. Basically what this means is that If you think you have an extremely high risk tolerance, there's a high chance you actually don't.

In addition, no one truly knows what their real risk tolerance is, until they actually go through a real market crash, and not just thinking out hypothetical situations in their head. As I showed in Chapter 2, historical data from the US stock market shows that the stock market can drop by over 40% in a single year. Can you stomach seeing your $100 portfolio drop to $50? Probably yes. But can you really stomach your hard earned portfolio 15 years into your investing journey, that drops from $500,000 to $250,000?

So then if you wanted to add bonds and have a percentage of your portfolio always at a set bond allocation, does this mean you would have to constantly monitor your stocks and bonds, and buy and sell constantly to make sure your portfolio always sticks to your set stock and bond percentages? Well no, you'd rebalance say once a year, and even then, it might not be necessary depending on the country you live in. In many countries, this is very easy nowadays, in that you can invest in funds provided by fund providers or banks, that set varying levels of allocations of stocks/bonds which then automatically rebalance as needed to remain at the

---

18 Brayman and Stipp. "Measurement of Client Risk Tolerance: How Improving Methodology Could Offer Advisors a Significant Competitive Advantage." Morningstar, 2021. https://www.morningstar.com/content/dam/marketing/northamerica/us/Products/Data_Research_Indexes/CLIENTRISK_2021_FIN2.pdf.

predefined allocations. It's a matter of choosing one based on your risk tolerance.

These are called asset allocation funds, and are increasingly available. They are simple all-in-one set it and forget it funds. The two biggest fund providers in the world are Vanguard and BlackRock, and they both have a large suite of funds that they offer in many countries, that are often tailored to the specific country. Asset allocation funds are often highly recommended for the average investor by investing communities, due to their simplicity and global diversification. The asset allocation funds usually hold underlying funds that track various global stock market indices, and as such, you'll basically have an asset allocation fund that is geographically diversified. You'll be primarily owning all the biggest, most successful, and most profitable companies all around the world. The underlying indices are self cleansing, and losers (underperforming companies) will be replaced with winners.

For example, in a hypothetical market-cap weighted index fund of two companies, if Company A has a market cap of $200, and Company B has a market cap of $800, that means that Company A will make up 20% of the index, while Company B makes up 80%. If you were to invest $100 in a fund that tracks these two companies, then $20 dollars would go into Company A, and $80 would go into Company B. At the same time, you'd own the same percentage of each company in a market cap-weighted fund, so in this case, $20 invested in Company A would be 10% ownership, and $80 invested in Company B would also be 10%. Therein lies the beauty of investing in index funds as summarized in the table that follows:

Example of a $100 Investment into a Hypothetical Market Cap-weighted Index Fund Tracking Two Companies

	Market Cap	Company Weight in the Index Fund (%)	Amount of Investment Going into Company	Ownership of Company (as % of Market Cap)
Company A	$200	20%	$20	10%
Company B	$800	80%	$80	10%
Total	$1000	100%	$100	

In terms of actual asset allocation funds available, the offerings are growing rapidly as more and more funds are created by more and more fund providers. For example, taking a look at what is available in Canada, most of the major fund providers/banks have an offering of very popular asset allocation funds designed to be core long-term holdings. For example, Vanguard Canada has the following asset allocation funds:

- **VEQT**[19]: 100% stocks / 0% bonds.
- **VGRO**: 80% stocks / 20% bonds.
- **VBAL**: 60% stocks / 40% bonds.
- **VCNS**: 40% stocks / 60% bonds.
- **VCIP**: 20% stocks / 80% bonds.

In general, asset allocation funds from fund providers are similar to the Vanguard funds I mentioned, where there are different funds that follow similar allocations of stocks/bonds, from higher risk 100/0, to roughly 20/80 on the other end of the risk spectrum. If we use historical US stocks and US 10-year bonds data, we can generate hypothetical funds with various

[19] VEQT etc. are the ticker symbols.

stocks/bonds percentages, and thus look at their hypothetical performance over 40 years[20]. We need to generate these hypothetical funds, because the actual currently offered asset allocation funds haven't been around for 40 years. Indeed not surprisingly, owning more stocks has performed better. We also see from the data that indeed that US stocks have historically had 10% annualized returns:

40-Year Performance of Hypothetical US Asset Allocation Funds (1980-2020)

	Fund (% US Stocks / US Bonds)			
	100 / 0	**80 / 20**	**60 / 40**	**40 / 60**
Annualized Return (%)	10.2	9.6	9.0	8.4
Standard Deviation (%)	15.2	12.4	10.2	9.0

If we look at the standard deviation, which is a measure of volatility in this context, then we see that as the percentage of stocks increases, so does the volatility. Stocks have higher expected returns, but also higher volatility. This is the reason why despite bonds having a lower expected return, people still do include bonds in their portfolio. While the individual risk tolerance is very personal, and I cannot advise you on that, one thing I did want to bring up is that you might want to

[20] The table has been produced by the author, using annual return data calculated by the author using raw data from the Shiller dataset, that serves as a proxy of overall US stock market performance, and a dataset of US bonds, both found in the public domain from the open source DataHub, which has explicitly released the data under the ODC Public Domain Dedication and License (PDDL).

consider picking an allocation strategy where even if it's not the most optimized for maximum return, if it's a strategy you can stick with without panic selling over an investing lifetime, then it might be worth it.

For example, if in theory, academically and mathematically, you would've made more money using a 100/0 portfolio, but instead you panic sold and realized losses throughout your investment lifetime, then it would actually be better to go with a less volatile portfolio, perhaps a 60/40 portfolio, but that you can stick with consistently over the long run. Remember in Chapter 2, I showed that even missing just the best 10 days in the stock market can potentially halve your returns. In a sense, for risk averse people, it could be better then for example to "only" have an annualized 7% return, than try a strategy that in theory would have yielded 10% returns but you would have lost money through panic selling.

Think of it as driving a car at 70 km/h (e.g. 80/20 portfolio) vs. 100 km/h (100% stocks), on a poorly maintained road with many bumps (stock market volatility). Both strategies get you where you need to go, but the 70 km/h drive can be less bumpy (less volatile) and less risk of crashing (panic selling/fear-driven decisions) for risk averse people. With this said, you may not want to go below 60% stocks, as you want enough growth to beat inflation and expenses as much as possible, to have enough money over the long term. I'll discuss this in the Retirement section of this chapter and why the 60% cut-off can be important.

While the table of data for the hypothetical asset allocation funds shows only about a 1% difference in the annualized return between the higher risk 100/0 vs. the more conservative 60/40 fund, it's important to note that this difference of 1% happens every year for 40 years, so it compounds. In an investment lifetime, this ends up being a substantial difference. Let's take a peek at the maths behind this, and look at a graph that shows someone who invests $10,000 per year, for 40 years, and the market either grows at 10% or 9% per year:

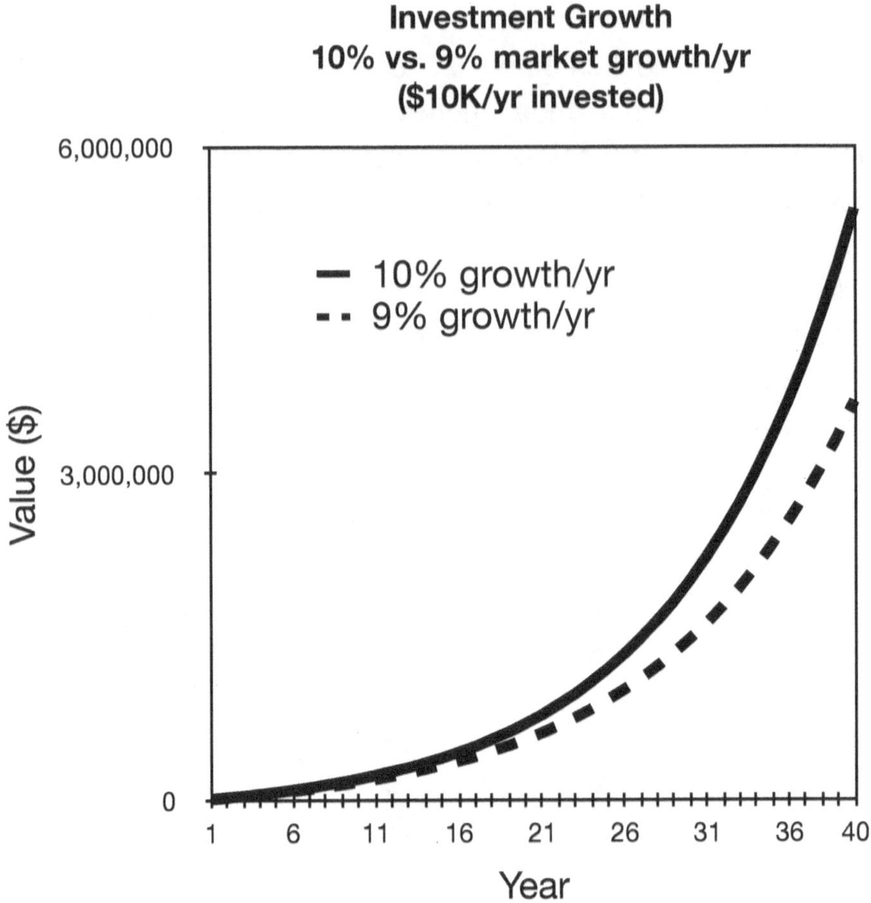

Hopefully now you can appreciate the impact a single percentage difference in annual growth makes. There is almost a $2,000,000 difference between the 100/0 vs. 60/40 funds by the end of the 40-year investment period.

Finally, asset allocation of stocks/bonds doesn't need to remain the same forever. Risk tolerance can change over time. One could start off in their 20s with a 100/0 setup, then move to an 80/20 when they hit 40, and then a 60/40 when they hit 60, just as an example of how one could potentially alter things as they get closer to retirement. But again, I reiterate the point that you may not want to go too low on the stocks percentage, specifically the 60% threshold. Although not common in Canada, other countries such as the US do have more offerings of TDFs (Target-Date Funds). TDFs are funds designed with a retirement year in mind, and they automatically adjust to reduce stocks and increase bonds as you get closer to retirement. They do often get very aggressive in the shift towards bonds as retirement approaches, which is something to evaluate in a TDF if you are interested in using one.

It's also important to point out here, that if you do go down the route of an asset allocation fund, it's best to pick an asset allocation fund that's offered by your local institutions, or one designed for your country by say Vanguard or BlackRock. This is because asset allocation funds can have a large home country bias, and can end up being overweight for domestic stocks. For example, it is recommended that Canadian investors hold roughly 30% Canadian and 70% international, although the Canadian stock market only makes up around 3% of the global stock market as a whole[21] i.e. a home bias. Reasons for a home bias are related to, among others, currency risk and geopolitical risk - because for most people, for the entirety of their investment lifetime, will be spending their home currency in their home country.

Indeed, the Vanguard Canada asset allocation funds I discussed previously include, for equities, roughly 30% allocation to Canada, and likewise it is roughly 30% as well for other Canadian asset allocation funds from BlackRock, TD, and BMO as examples. Hence it's important to choose the appropriate fund either from your country or tailored to your country. It makes no sense to be overweight on Canadian stocks for example, if you live in Australia, and vice-versa - you'd not be benefiting from the home bias. Home bias aside,

[21] Vanguard. "Canadians Reducing Home Bias, Eh? Vanguard Research Finds That Investors Are Increasingly Going Global." 2023.

a roughly 30% domestic/70% international portfolio may also be an optimal portfolio based on recent investment lifecycle research, which will be discussed in the Retirement section at the end of this chapter.

If you are in a country where Vanguard, BlackRock, or your local institutions don't offer an all-in-one globally diversified asset allocation fund, then indeed you will need to put together your own, and rebalance according to your set schedule. For example, this was the case in Canada just a few short years ago. When I started investing back in 2016, we had to build our own portfolios using low cost individual funds. For example, there was a time when people managed a 4-fund portfolio, with low-cost mutual funds (the "e-series" mutual funds) from TD bank (a big bank in Canada) that included four separate individual funds tracking the USA, Canada, rest of world (excluding US/CAN), and an e-series bond mutual fund. In such a case, people would indeed manually rebalance annually, so that the proportions of the funds would remain at their predefined allocation weightings. Nowadays the fund providers and banks are constantly increasing their offerings around the world, so there'll be more all-in-one set it and forget it funds as time goes on.

For the Americans reading this, who represent a large portion of the personal finance community, an example of a popular and well known all-stocks US-tailored fund, would be the Vanguard Total World (ticker symbol VT). VT is market-cap weighted and currently comprised of roughly 60% US stocks/ 40% rest of world stocks. A complementary bond fund would be Vanguard Total Bond (ticker symbol BND).

Geography

So now we've covered asset classes, it's time to move on to geography. As I already mentioned, there are now asset allocation funds that diversify globally. These funds would basically be the tools that are available for you to invest globally (or you put together your own if your country doesn't have any asset allocation fund offerings). As mentioned, these globally diversified asset allocation funds are highly recommended within the investing community. They're a simple all in one, and for average investors, you want to be diversified. If you're in Canada, you can pick one of the funds from Vanguard that I've discussed previously or one from any of the major providers (Appendix 2 has a list for Canadians). Likewise if you live elsewhere, providers such as Vanguard and BlackRock have created funds tailored to many countries around the world. But let's talk about the data that supports this view of global diversification.

At the moment of writing this book, many people in various online investment communities talk of investing only in VOO or VFV (S&P 500 ETFs) because of the belief in US exceptionalism and their continued outperformance. This view however, may be due to recency bias. In the most recent decade for which we have complete performance data on (so the 2010s), the US for example vastly outperformed the Canadian stock market.

This is shown in the graph that follows, which depicts the hypothetical growth of $10,000 invested in various decades in either the US or Canadian stock market[22]. However, if we look at the decade prior to the 2010s, so the 2000s, a $10,000 investment in the US market in 2000, would have ended up at

[22] The graph showing growth of $10,000 has been created by the author, using annual return data calculated by the author, using raw data in the public domain. For the US stock market, raw data used was from the Shiller dataset that serves as a proxy of overall US stock market performance, found in the public domain from the open source DataHub, which has explicitly released the data under the ODC Public Domain Dedication and License (PDDL); and for the Canada stock market from the Government of Canada (Statistics Canada. Table 10-10-0125-01 Toronto Stock Exchange statistics), released under the Open Government License (OGL).

the end of the decade (2010) roughly still at $10,000. This is because the US stock market had a decade of stagnation. Whereas Canada's stock market on the other hand, had an annualized return of roughly 4.5%.

In fact, both the US and Canada outperformed each other in an equal amount of decades from the 1960s to the 2010s, with each having three decades of outperforming the other. The fact is that there will always be times where for example the US market was stagnant (e.g. 2000 to 2010), and in that same period another country's stock market actually grew. There will always be periods where certain countries perform better than others, and no one can predict who will perform the best in the future. With this in mind and the data from the graph, it would seem most logical to diversify globally. As such, asset allocation funds that are globally diversified are indeed a good long-term core holding for the average investor.

US vs. Canada Stock Market: Hypothetical Growth of $10,000 Invested in Various Decades

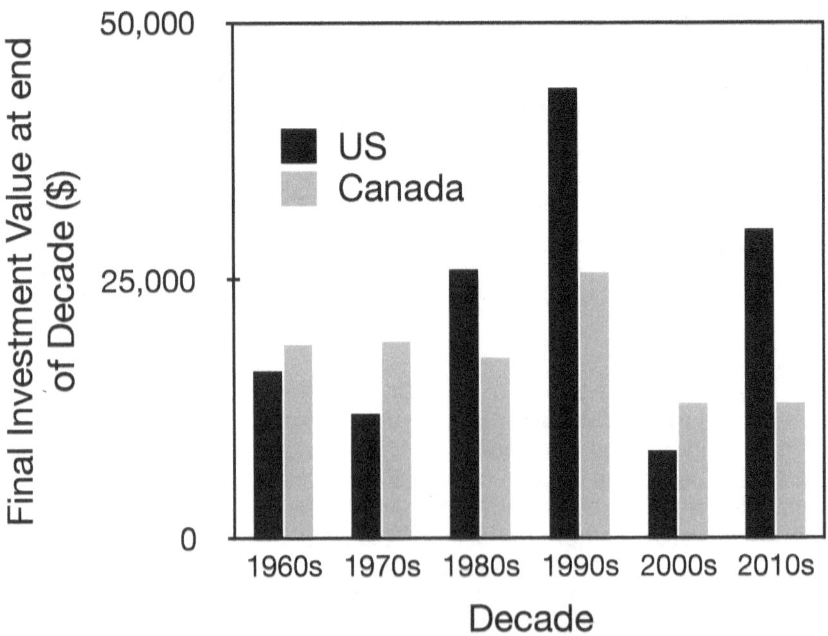

Costs

So now we have discussed asset allocation in terms of asset class and geography, and the fact that there are now all-in-one simple, globally diversified, asset allocation funds, then that's the end of the story, right? Well not quite. They say that the only free lunch in investing is diversification. The fact that all these fund providers and banks have constructed and will manage these simple beautiful asset allocation funds, well, it obviously comes with a price tag. Companies won't just do this all for you for free, they charge fees, specifically what's known as a MER (Management Expense Ratio). You won't have to actively pay this fee, it comes off the funds performance each year.

For example, if you bought a S&P 500 index fund with a 0.5% MER, and the S&P 500 index itself went up 10% that year, your return would only be 9.5% for that year. You can't control geopolitics, pandemics, wars, and the economy, but one thing you can control is keeping costs low, and that's by looking at fees. Now a couple of percentage in fees might seem like nothing much, but it has a much bigger impact than you think. Many institutions offer funds, in particular actively managed mutual funds, in which the fee can be a 2-3% MER. It's worth mentioning here that often times in online investing communities, people will say that mutual funds have high fees, and index funds have low fees and you should go for index funds. Now, this isn't actually entirely correct, for a few reasons:

1. First of all, an index fund is a fund that tracks an index. If a mutual fund tracks an index such as the S&P 500, it is also an index fund.
2. Not all mutual funds are actively managed (see point 1 above) and not all mutual funds have high fees.

3. Mutual funds themselves are not inherently bad, actively managed, nor have high fees.

With that out of the way, let's look at the impact of fees, using the example of someone starting off with $5,000, and consistently contributing an additional $5,000 each year into funds with different MERs, for 35 years, at a 10% return per year. As you can see from the graph that follows, there isn't too much of a difference between the funds that had a MER around 0.2-0.5%, which is a common fee range for most asset allocation funds and index funds (though many funds in the US have even lower fees), as they're just mostly passively tracking the index and there's not much a fund manager needs to do.

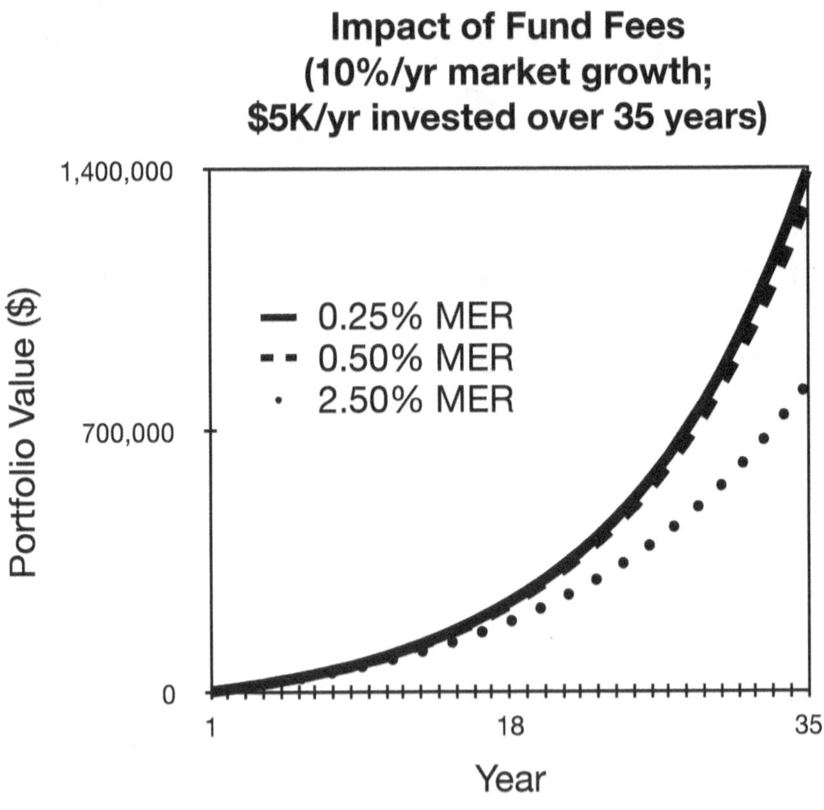

On the other hand, we can see a dramatic impact on the final portfolio value for funds that would have fees anywhere between 2-3%, almost halving the final value. 2-3% is a common MER for actively managed funds. These funds, managed by professionals, often have themes (such as targeting specific sectors etc.) and the idea is that such active strategies could potentially outperform the index funds/general market. However, it has been found that almost 90% of professional fund managers don't outperform the general market[23]. Even for the actively managed funds that matched the market, or even beat the market a bit, once the high fees are accounted for, you'd still likely end up underperforming the market. The best bet for the average person is asset allocation or index funds with low fees. When picking these funds, all else being equal, try to go for the ones with fees no higher than 0.5% MER at most - the lower the better.

No matter in the end what asset allocation strategy (stocks/bonds breakdown and geography) and fund you choose, the absolute key is to pick a percentage of your income you can afford to invest, and decide on a contribution schedule (e.g. fortnightly or monthly) and consistently stick to it. Try to aim for anywhere between 5-25% of your salary to invest each year. Even if it means starting off at a lower percentage, the key is just to get started and be consistent. In addition, reinvest your dividend payouts so they compound too. Many brokerages allow you to automate your investment contributions and dividend reinvestments (commonly known as DRIP) now as well. Remember that as I showed in the graphs in Chapter 2, compounding and time is a big factor, even in the scenario where it was someone investing only 5% each year of

[23] Levy, A. "You Can Outperform 88% of Professional Fund Managers by Using This Simple Investment Strategy." The Motley Fool, 2024. https://www.fool.com/investing/2024/06/29/you-can-outperform-88-of-professional-fund-manager/

a below average salary. Finally, by consistently keeping to a contribution schedule, you will also allow yourself to buy stocks on a “discount”, if you are able to maintain consistency throughout recessions and market corrections.

Picking individual stocks

So, now we’re set to go, right? But you, or at least many people if not you specifically, are wondering, well if I buy a globally diversified asset allocation fund, I’d only be average, I’d basically grow with how the overall market grows? Well yes, you’d be *Averagely Rich*. And you’re probably wondering why you can’t just pick individual home-run companies that are the next Apple or Microsoft, right? Well, if only it were that simple. If we take a look at the top 10 companies in the S&P 500 over the decades looking at the table that follows[24,25], what we see is that the list is constantly changing. The “winners” can change quickly, which makes it extremely difficult to pick the right companies. Today’s “winner” may be tomorrow's “loser”.

---

24 Oppenhimer P, S Bell, L Peytavin, and G Jaisson. “Global Strategy Paper 25 Years on; Lessons from the Bursting of the Technology Bubble.” Goldman Sachs Portfolio Research Strategy, 2025. https://www.goldmansachs.com/pdfs/insights/goldman-sachs-research/25-years-on-lessons-from-the-bursting-of-the-tech-bubble/redaction.pdf

25 The companies that make up the S&P 500 are a matter of public record. The table was created by the author, using a list of S&P 500 companies from the publicly available 2025 Goldman Sachs Portfolio Research study. S&P 500® is a registered trademark of S&P Dow Jones Indices LLC. All work (graphs, tables, text) in this book that references any of Standard & Poor’s is not affiliated with or endorsed by S&P Dow Jones Indices LLC.

Top 10 S&P 500 Companies from 1985-2024

	1985	1990	1995	2000
1	IBM	IBM	General Electric	General Electric
2	Exxon Mobil	Exxon Mobil	AT&T	Exxon Mobil
3	General Electric	General Electric	Exxon Mobil	Pfizer
4	Philip Morris	Philip Morris	Coca-Cola	Cisco Systems
5	General Motors	Royal Dutch Shell	Merck & Co	Citigroup
6	Amoco	Bristo-Myers Squibb	Philip Morris	Walmart
7	Royal Duch Shell	Merck & Co	Royal Dutch Shell	Microsoft
8	Du Pont	Walmart	Procter & Gamble	AIG
9	AT&T	AT&T	Johnson & Johnson	Merck & Co
10	Chevron	Coca-Cola	IBM	Intel
	2005	**2010**	**2015**	**2024**
1	General Electric	Exxon Mobil	Apple	Apple
2	Exxon Mobil	Apple	Alphabet	Nvidia
3	Citigroup	Microsoft	Microsoft	Microsoft
4	Microsoft	General Electric	Exxon Mobil	Alphabet
5	Procter & Gamble	Chevron	General Electric	Amazon.com
6	Bank of America	IBM	Johnson & Johnson	Meta Platforms
7	Johnson & Johnson	Procter & Gamble	Amazon.com	Eli Lilly
8	AIG	AT&T	Wells Fargo	Broadcom
9	Pfizer	Johnson & Johnson	Berkshire Hathaway	Tesla
10	Philip Morris	JPMorgan Chase	JPMorgan Chase	JPMorgan Chase

I still remember when AIM (AOL Instant Messenger) was so popular in the 90s, the incredible pioneering and exciting days of the early internet era. I'm sure at that moment, people would think that AOL would be around forever and we'd always be talking to friends on AIM, and IBM PCs would be the computers we'd always be using. Well fast forward to today, and AOL no longer exists as an independent company, and IBM no longer makes PCs, and neither are in the top 10 of the S&P 500 anymore. Today, Facebook Messenger, WhatsApp, and Apple iMessage have taken over the IM space; and companies like Apple, Dell, and Lenovo dominate the PC space. If we look a bit more into the S&P 500, and not just how the list of top companies change over time, we see that the majority of the increase in the US stock market can come from a very small number of companies. For example, research from J.P. Morgan Wealth Management[26], found that in 2023, just seven companies (the Magnificent 7[27]) accounted for 60% of the S&P 500 index's gains. This means that roughly 1% of the companies in the index can account for a very significant portion of market gains. Unless you're smart enough to find the next 1% of the top companies, you'd better stick to index fund investing in the long run.

In fact, a study in 2024, which looked at the performance of all publicly listed company stocks in the US over roughly a century (almost 30,000 companies), showed that the majority of stocks lost money, specifically 52% of stocks had negative cumulative returns[28]. Meaning that if someone had bought

---

[26] Ausenbaugh E. "Quick Shot: Anatomy of the Rally: Is the Stock Market's Performance Concentrated in Just a Few Names?" J.P. Morgan Wealth Management, 2024. https://static.chasecdn.com/content/articles/article-library/en/tmt-february-twenty-seven-twenty-four-daily.public.html

[27] The Magnificent 7 is comprised of Alphabet, Amazon, Apple, Meta, Microsoft, Nvidia, and Tesla.

[28] Bessembinder H. "Which U.S. Stocks Generated the Highest Long-Term Returns?" SSRN, 2024. https://doi.org/10.2139/ssrn.4897069

company stock at the time of listing and held (with dividends reinvested even), until the stock was delisted or until the end of the study sampling period (31 December 2023), they would have lost money in 52% of companies that they invested in.

Investing is meant to be boring. Successful investing is meant to be even more boring. But if you really have the itch to try and pick some winners, then be disciplined enough to always set a hard limit. For example, you never invest an amount that's more than 5% of your total portfolio, into individual stocks, and you make sure you keep to your rule. I always remind myself to stick to globally diversified funds and to consistently invest and remain invested, by telling myself that timing the market doesn't require you to be just right, it needs you to be right twice! You need to be able to sell at the peak, and buy back in at the bottom.

3: Retirement

The wealth building phase can be looked at as actually quite simple and general for everyone, compared to retirement. You want to build wealth as much as possible in a consistent, risk adjusted manner with diversification. Made even simpler now with index funds and globally diversified asset allocation funds. Retirement is different - how can you be sure you won't run out of money, do you want to leave anything behind, or do you want to die with zero? How do you want to spend your retirement years? Do you want to give money away during your retirement? There's a lot of personal decisions to make, and it's much more complex in a sense than during the wealth building phase. I guess one big question really comes down to how much can you withdraw every year in retirement, in order to spend as much as you can on what you want, but not so much that your retirement portfolio "fails" i.e. you run out of money and you're still alive.

Studies have looked into this, the most famous being the seminal 1998 Trinity study[29] conducted by three Trinity University professors. The study showed that there was a 95% success rate for not exhausting (running out of money) one's portfolio at a 4% withdrawal rate - known as the 4% rule. This held only if there were at least 50% US stocks in the portfolio, over a 30-year retirement. This is also why earlier above, I recommended to go no more conservative than the 60/40 stocks/bonds asset allocation funds, as once you start going below the ~60% stocks threshold, you may start losing out to inflation and run the high risk of running out of money. Once stocks drop below that 50% threshold, and bonds exceed 50%, the failure rates dramatically increase as shown in the data from the Trinity study, summarized in the table that follows.

The 30-year retirement in the study is not based on a single 30 year period in history, but rather, the study used rolling 30-year periods between 1926 and 1995, like the Cresmont study I discussed in Chapter 2 that showed there was no 20-year period where the S&P 500 would've lost money. In the Trinity study, they started with the first 30 year period from 1926 to 1955, and then the next 30 year period from 1927 to 1956, and so on until the last possible 30 year period starting in 1966 and ending in 1995. Five portfolios of various stocks/bonds allocations were then tested across all these 30-year periods, to determine the number of periods in which each portfolio would fail (run out of money).

With regards to the withdrawal rates, a 5% withdrawal rate already significantly increases the failure rate, to where anything at that rate and beyond is not worth considering for most people (the study itself goes up to much higher percentages, but I did not include them in the summary table

[29] Cooley PL, Hubbard CM, and Walz DT. "Retirement Savings: Choosing a Withdrawal Rate That Is Sustainable." AAII JOURNAL, 1998. https://www.aaii.com/journal/199802/feature.pdf

that follows[30], as it's a bit of a moot point). A common misconception relates to what the 4% rule actually means. The 4% rule is not 4% of your portfolio value withdrawn every year, it's 4% only in the first year of retirement, with the subsequent years adjusted for inflation. The study isn't calling for a fixed 4% withdrawal, but rather a fixed 4% withdrawal *of real dollars*. When the adjustment for inflation is made, it is not adjusting from the total portfolio value, but adjusting the initial withdrawal amount itself. For example, you started off with a $1,000,000 portfolio, and in your first year you withdraw $40,000 (i.e. 4%). If inflation is 2% the next year, you would therefore withdraw $40,800 (i.e. $40,000 x 1.02). This means that the portfolio value itself is not taken into account, which essentially can contribute to portfolio failure.

Trinity Study: Inflation-Adjusted Portfolio Success Rates for a 30-Year Retirement

Percentage of Stocks / Bonds	**Withdrawal Rate as a % of portfolio value at the start of retirement**			
	3%	**4%**	**5%**	**6%**
100 / 0	100	*95*	85	68
75 / 25	100	*98*	83	68
50 / 50	100	*95*	76	51
25 / 75	100	71	27	20
0 / 100	80	20	17	12

Retirement is not static, and it's a dynamic process. No

30 Table produced by the author, and uses data adapted from the Trinity paper referenced.

one that was smart enough to build a portfolio and be consistent to get to the place of having a portfolio for retirement, would be stupid enough to plan their spending decades in advance and then blindly follow that plan regardless of the performance of their portfolio. It would be unfathomable that such an intelligent person that got here, is now starting in retirement with a plan to blindly spend their way to bankruptcy. It's important to note here then, that the Trinity study is an academic and mathematical exercise, and nowhere in the study have the authors claimed that you must use a 4% withdrawal rate, nor do they say you must keep the withdrawal rate consistent.

Portfolio failure occurs in large part due to SORR (Sequence of Return Risk). SORR is the risk that the order in which investment returns occur negatively affects your portfolio's outcome. For example, you retire, and the stock market crashes, or it crashes in the second or third year, basically pretty soon after your retirement. This is where logic and common sense comes in, and one must account for SORR and stock market down years. For one, withdrawal does not exactly need to track inflation, it just depends on what you need. While you may have had to withdraw 4% in your first year of retirement, it could've just been because you had a large expense, and that your portfolio is of such a size that 1% could have met your usual every day expenses. In such a case, in your second year of retirement, if the stock market were to crash, you wouldn't then do another 4% withdrawal, since you want to be accounting for the SORR, and at the same time, you don't even need 4% of your portfolio to meet your necessities.

Another question is whether the 4% rule even applies to you? Say you have a $8,000,000 portfolio by the time you hit retirement. 4% would be $320,000 - do you even need that much in any year in retirement? Again, one must withdraw in a way that accounts for their individual actual needs, and in addition to be as flexible as possible to account for the dynamic nature of the stock markets performance.

To further extend on this Trinity study, a more recent 2023 Lifecycle study from three professors at three different academic institutes, has looked at the entire lifetime (i.e. investment lifecycle) of an investor, from starting at age 25, all the way up to retirement at 65, until death, also using a 4% withdrawal rate in retirement[31]. In this study, the base case for the hypothetical "investor" was:

- A US couple comprised of a male and female, and the same age.
- They start with no wealth.
- Started investing at 25, investing 10% of their annual salary, and stopping at 65 (so 40 years of investment contributions).
- A 4% withdrawal rate of *real dollars* (i.e. same as the Trinity study, in which the withdrawal amount is adjusted each year for inflation).
- Availability of US spousal and survivor benefits.

This Lifecycle study was extremely elegant in my opinion, and differed from the Trinity study and the Crestmont analysis of the S&P 500, where instead of using rolling 20 or 30 year periods, they used a block bootstrap resampling statistical method. Using this procedure, they randomly pieced together roughly 10-year blocks (the years within the blocks are sequential years) to simulate different hypothetical scenarios that didn't actually occur in real life.

For example, they could have pieced together blocks in the order of a 1920s block, followed by a 1950s block, and then a

[31] Anarkulova A, Cederburg S, and O'Doherty M. "Beyond the Status Quo: A Critical Assessment of Lifecycle Investment Advice." SSRN Electronic Journal, 2023. https://doi.org/10.2139/ssrn.4590406

2010s block, essentially simulating as if someone was investing starting from the Great Depression, then jumps to the post WW2 boom, and then jumps to the post global financial crisis boom. Likewise, they could have pieced together blocks that went from 1920s, then to 2010s, then to 1950s, meaning in this simulation, someone would have invested starting from the Great Depression, then jumps to the post global financial crisis boom, followed by the post WW2 boom. By doing so, they could test various investment portfolio strategies across many different simulations, and not limited to only what happened in history. The dataset used included historical data for stocks, government bonds, and government bills spanning over 2,600 years of country-month data from 39 developed countries. While the data availability for each country differed, in totality the data spanned from 1890 to 2023.

In addition to simulating different time-period scenarios, the study also simulated different scenarios to account for:

- Varying income that aims to fit varying lifecycle earnings data on millions of US workers from the US Social Security Act. In the simulations, the workers income peaked in their 40s, with simulated median income at roughly $70K, valued in 2022 US dollars. Income simulations incorporate US Social Security and Supplemental Security Income during retirement.
- An individual may experience unemployment, and no investment contributions are made during unemployment.
- Individuals earning less than $15,000 (in 2022 US dollars) in any given year, will not make contributions.
- Different ages of death in retirement for both partners, including one dying earlier first.
- Possibility of death of one or both partners even before age 65.
- Took into account longevity risk, by looking at Social Security

data, and accounting for the fact that at the 95th percentile, there are individuals that live till 100.

In doing so, they simulated 1,000,000 different hypothetical scenarios! The study looked at different portfolio strategies and how they would perform in the various simulations. The portfolios were held by the investor throughout their *entire* investment lifecycle, so right from the beginning (25 years of age) all the way through to and including retirement, and finally death. What the study found, was that an all stocks portfolio had the greatest chance of "success" (not running out of money in retirement before the death of the last survivor of the couple), and specifically the Optimal Portfolio was 33% domestic stocks and 67% international stocks[32].

Lifecycle Study: Failure Probability of Portfolios Across 1,000,000 Simulations for Households (using 4% Withdrawal Rate in retirement)

Portfolio	Probability of Failure (%)
Optimal Portfolio (all stocks) (33% domestic / 67% international)	6.7
Balanced Portfolio (60/40 stocks/bonds)	16.9
All stocks domestic	17.1
Target-date fund	19.7
Bills (short term government-debt, like a short term "bond")	38.9

[32] Table produced by the author using data adapted from the referenced paper: Beyond the Status Quo: A Critical Assessment of Lifecycle Investment Advice

Although the base case investor was a US couple, the Optimal Portfolio is not US-specific, and the analysis of portfolio performance extended to the 39 developed countries included in the study. Apart from the US, 33% domestic stocks would indeed be a "home bias", which I discussed earlier in the Strategy section, where funds often have an overweight allocation to the home country stocks for various advantageous reasons. In the Optimal Portfolio, the probability of failure (running out of money in retirement before the death of both partners) was only 6.7%.

This is not surprising, as it echoes a similar conclusion to the Trinity study, and the available historical stocks and bonds data. Since stocks have a higher expected return than bonds, it's not surprising that with less stocks and more bonds, the failure rate is higher. By having more stocks, and having a long-term horizon to drown out the "noise" (ups and downs/ volatility), you begin to sail towards the smoother roughly 10% annual returns of the stock market. As such, with 100% stocks, you'd have a greater chance of beating out inflation and expenses, and having more real dollars throughout a long-term investment lifecycle, compared to less stocks and having more bonds (which have had long-term real returns of only about 1% annually[33]).

It's also worth noting the high probability of failure of the target-date fund at almost 20%. I mentioned in the Strategy section previously that they do usually shift towards bonds pretty aggressively as retirement approaches. The low real returns of bonds could indeed put target-date funds at risk of failure in retirement. This study used a hypothetical target-date fund that was meant to be representative of the popular real world offerings.

---

[33] Anarkulova A, Cederburg S, and O'Doherty M. "Beyond the Status Quo: A Critical Assessment of Lifecycle Investment Advice." SSRN Electronic Journal, 2023. https://doi.org/10.2139/ssrn.4590406

Again, however, the Lifecycle study is academic in nature, and is showing a point mathematically. Certain assumptions are made in this study, which present slight caveats, for example the "investor" in the study starts investing at 25. Many people such as scientists and physicians may still be studying and training at 25, with debt and not investing. True retirement, as I mentioned previously in the chapter, doesn't need to have a 4% withdrawal rate to begin with, nor do you need to have a fixed percentage withdrawal of real dollars that you need to stick with regardless of market performance in retirement. Retirement is dynamic, and you will need to plan accordingly to your situation at the time based on how much money you'll actually need in a given year, with flexibility to account for market corrections.

As we draw near to the closing chapter of the book, in terms of a final definitive recommendation of a portfolio for anyone reading, that's something I can't give you. At most, all I can say is a diversified stock portfolio is what I believe in and what I use - very similar to the Optimal Portfolio from the Lifecycle study actually. Risk is complex and the exact asset allocation portfolio that's right for you, will need you to carefully think about with yourself, and to discuss with your financial advisor as needed. What I can tell you is that there's two broad risks to consider:

- There is the risk of volatility causing panic selling, which is often talked about, in which adding a bond component is commonly recommended.
- Then on the other hand, as the Trinity and Lifecycle studies have shown, there is also the other risk (and perhaps even more important risk) of running out of money, which would point towards having a higher allocation to stocks to have the highest chance possible of beating out inflation in the long run.

In the end, time in the market is the most important, and time and compounding are two of the biggest drivers of investment success. If you are stuck with analysis paralysis on how to get started in terms of stocks/bonds percentages, then it might be worthwhile to think of a middle ground and discussing perhaps a balanced approach with your financial advisor.

If you haven't started yet, that means you're new to investing, and it's hard to know your true risk tolerance, and for inexperienced investors, panic selling could definitely happen. So perhaps a 100/0 (stocks/bonds) is too volatile for you? On the other hand, you don't want to run the risk of not beating inflation enough and running out of money in the long run, so perhaps the 60/40 portfolio is too conservative? In that sense, an 80/20 portfolio could be the balanced middle ground approach, and something that you can bring up when you next meet your financial advisor.

Remember, whatever you decide on, you're not stuck with it forever. Strategies can change, and people's risk tolerance as well, especially as time goes on and one experiences different ups and downs in the markets. In the end, whatever path you gravitate towards, remember to be diversified - that's the only free lunch in investing.

CHAPTER 4
FINAL THOUGHTS

I hope that the journey to get to the end of this book has been enjoyable, and that you appreciated the data-driven approach to address the common questions and topics in investing. I also hope that you can see how today, it is extremely easy to get started on your investment journey, and the costs are incredibly low and the tools are very accessible. In the end, for me personally, what I have learnt the most from my investment journey of roughly a decade, is that the most important things are starting as early as possible, be emotionally patient and let compounding do its job. One thing I also learnt along the way that was extremely valuable that I haven't mentioned in the book previously, is that while it's important to avoid lifestyle creep and control spending, it's also important to enjoy life and spend to have some fun - balance the two since you only live once.

Again, I wanted to reiterate what I mentioned in the beginning, and that is this book is being told from the perspective of when I wrote the book, which was the summer of 2025. There are the specifics such as the research papers I discussed which may or may not apply anymore, years later when you might read this book. But in saying that, the general principles and the fundamentals of the stock market (such as diversification, patience, time and compounding) I discussed will always be relevant.

Apart from the lessons above, the remaining important lesson extends on being properly diversified. It's incredibly difficult if not impossible for the average retail investor to beat the market. The Efficient Market Hypothesis is the theory that all available information about companies is fully reflected in the asset prices[34], implying that one can't beat the market, and the Modern Portfolio Theory is that that diversification can eliminate idiosyncratic (unsystematic) risk[35] such as single company risk. Putting the two together, it indicates that the best path to investing is by owning a globally diversified fund. While I find it hard to believe that the market is always totally efficient, due to people investing based on fear and emotions, not all information being correct, or not all information being available, I do believe that the market is mostly efficient most of the time.

I wanted to finish off the book by circling back to Chapter 1, and re-addressing the main points for both the barriers to starting, and the most important pillars once you've started:

"I invested in stocks but it hasn't really gone up much": **Investing is long term, let compounding do its job.**

"I invested but then the stocks went down": **The market is volatile in the short term, but in the long run, markets have historically returned around 10% a year on average. The S&P 500 thus far has never had a 20-year period where you would've lost money.**

"I don't know how": **It's simpler than ever now with online brokerages either with your bank or online discount brokerages, and the availability of index funds and all-in-one asset allocation funds.**

---

[34] Fama, Eugene F. "Efficient Capital Markets: II." The Journal of Finance 46, no. 5 (1991): 1575–617. https://doi.org/10.1111/j.1540-6261.1991.tb04636.x.

[35] Markowitz, Harry. "Portfolio Selection." The Journal of Finance 7, no. 1 (1952): 77. https://doi.org/10.2307/2975974.

"I don't have money": **There are now online discount brokerages that offer commission-free and fractional-trading options. You can start small, even if you can only afford to invest $1 a month, just get started.**

The best time to start investing was when you were 18-25, and the second best time is today. We live in a world where there are incredible opportunities. While the world as a whole is not perfect, and neither is capitalism and the free market, the purpose of my book was not to portray it all as being perfect and not to teach you how you can become a millionaire or get rich quick. But rather, to show you that in the world we live in today, it certainly is possible for you to grow up in a family that was around the poverty line, to then improve things somewhat in your adult life, at least in terms of finances. Essentially, we do have the possibility to go from poverty in one generation, to being middle-class, comfortable and well off enough to not worry about whether you can afford food for the week in the next generation.

With this said, I certainly don't want to dismiss the challenges that many do face and how it could be challenging for certain individuals, especially individuals faced with not just one great challenge of either poverty, political oppression, war, health issues/disabilities or the likes, but facing several at the same time. I mentioned in the preface that one of my motivations for writing this book, was my personal journey of growing up poor in social housing, to landing in the middle class as an adult, and that I really wanted to let people know that did grow up poor like me, that it is possible to find a way out and up.

But, luck still has a lot to do with everything. Growing up, I experienced poverty, but did not have to face poverty alongside additional struggles such as health issues/political oppression/war or whatever else, as many others do experience today. It's not as simple sometimes to tell people in these situations to "hustle" and "pull yourself up by your bootstraps", and I'm very well aware of this and also the imperfections of the world we live in. But it is still worth trying your best to be the best you can possibly be. Everyday you're alive is a day something incredible could happen.

In your journey, it's important to remember that life is meant to be enjoyed and you're meant to have fun, otherwise what's the point? Specifically, for your finance journey, you'll need to take it seriously as managing healthy personal finances is so important, but not at the expense of not having any fun in life. It's a delicate balance, and that part's up to you. Money absolutely is important, but money is not the most important thing in life.

“You can't make an omelette without breaking eggs. You have a system which is overwhelmingly yielding good results, but there’s no question that it's not perfect and there are cases and people will get hurt, but that's true of any system.” - Milton Friedman

"A man's right to work as he will, to spend what he earns, to own property, to have the state as servant and not as master, they are the essence of a free economy, and on that freedom all our other freedoms depend." - Margaret Thatcher.

"Science and everyday life cannot and should not be separated. Science, for me, gives a partial explanation of life. In so far as it goes, it is based on fact, experience and experiment" - Rosalind Franklin

APPENDIX 1
CANADIAN ACCOUNT TYPES

The appendices apply only to Canadians, so you can skip this part if you want if you're not Canadian. So at the beginning of Chapter 3, I discussed opening a brokerage. For Canada (and likely in your country too if you're not Canadian), you can not only open a "regular" (i.e. non-registered) account, but you can also open an account at a brokerage that is tax-sheltered, which is very important for Canadians. There are tools that allow your investments to grow tax-free. I'm sure most of you have heard of these:

- TFSA (Tax Free Savings Account).
- RRSP (Registered Retirement Savings Plan).
- FHSA (First Home Savings Account).
- RESP (Registered Education Savings Plan).

You probably use these accounts by opening them up as actual bank deposit savings accounts, earning the typical (low) interest rates. But did you know they can also be used for investing? Because you can actually open a brokerage account type that is either a TFSA, RRSP, FHSA, or RESP. Perhaps the word "savings" in these account type names doesn't do them enough justice. They're not just for savings deposits at your bank for earning typical interest. You can also use them to own stocks in and use them for investing.

1: TFSA

The TFSA allows you to invest your money that grows tax free *and* is not taxed upon withdrawal. It is an extremely powerful tool that can be used for any goals and not just retirement. It can be opened by anyone at their age of maturity for their province (so 18 or 19). The TFSA started in 2009, and each year, the government dictates an annual contribution room. The additional contribution room each year is subject to change and usually adjusted for inflation. If any contribution room is unused, it will be carried forward indefinitely. Your contribution room starts accumulating the year you turn 18. As such, if you were 18 in 2009, and haven't used your TFSA, you would have all the annual contribution room possible as your total contribution limit. Unused contribution room carries forward indefinitely, even if you have not opened an account yet. An important point is if you are an immigrant and arrived in Canada after 2009 - you will not have the full possible contribution limit even if you were 18 in 2009, but rather, it'll be calculated from the year you arrived in Canada. An important point to remember is to not over contribute (contribute over your total limit) in any given year, otherwise there are penalties.

If you make a withdrawal, note that the contribution room is not added back to your contribution limit until the first day of the following year. For example, if you had a $10,000 total contribution limit in 2020, and you moved $10,000 from your bank account into your brokerage TFSA, to invest in an index fund, then you're contribution room is gone for that year. Even if you withdrew $5,000 some time in 2020, you can't add $5,000 back into your TFSA in that year, as you would be penalized on a $5,000 over contribution. Your $5,000 contribution room will be added back on the first day of the following year however, as any withdrawals in a TFSA will have the total of those amounts added back onto the contribution limit on the first day of the following year. So in this example of $5,000 withdrawal in 2020, if the government set the contribution room for 2021 as $10,000, then you'd have a total contribution limit of $15,000 in 2021 ($10,000 government set amount in 2021 + the $5,000 you withdrew in 2020).

2: RRSP

The RRSP also allows your money to grow tax free, just like the TFSA, and is designed to be for retirement goals. Unlike the TFSA though, the contribution room requires you to have earned income first, and the room each year is based on 18% of the previous year's earned income (up to a government defined maximum), reduced by any pension contributions (from work pension plans or work defined contributions). For example, if your work contributed 6% of your salary for your work group retirement plan, a pension adjustment will take this amount into account in the *following* year's contribution limit. Like the TFSA, any unused contribution room carries over indefinitely. Again, there is a penalty for over contribution.

The RRSP does, however, differ from the TFSA in a big way upon withdrawal, in which withdrawals are taxed according to your income bracket at the time of withdrawal. This is because you are essentially contributing "pre-tax" dollars into your RRSP. Although you are technically contributing your already taxed money, the amount you contribute is tax deductible, and can result in a tax return. For example:

- Income: $80,000
- RRSP Contribution: $10,000
- Taxable income becomes: $70,000

In this example, you pay tax as if you only made $70,000,

not $80,000. If you are to take advantage of contributing and investing within your RRSP, to make it really snowball and be worthwhile, you want to reinvest back to your RRSP any tax return as a result of contributing to your RRSP. Your tax return is not free money, you're merely deferring paying tax.

Because of this, the RRSP is extremely powerful if you are in a high income bracket, and expect to retire at a lower income bracket (because you'll likely spend less in retirement). You defer paying tax on income that otherwise would be taxed at your "high" income tax bracket in your working years, and instead will now pay tax on it at a "low" income tax bracket when you withdraw in retirement.

You can keep the RRSP open until at the very latest age 71, in which it must be either closed down and everything withdrawn (generally not recommended as you'll be taxed on the entire amount), or convert it into an income producing source such as a RRIF (Registered Retirement Income Fund) or annuity. Once you reach this stage, a minimum amount needs to be withdrawn each year, which are percentages set by the government and change over time. You will need to determine what the minimum withdrawals are at the time you personally retire and reach 71.

The RRSP can also be withdrawn tax-free to buy your first home, up to a certain amount set by the government, which has changed over time - right now it's $60,000, but you will need to check at the time you decide to withdraw from your RRSP under the First Home Buyers plan. The amount withdrawn does need to be paid back within 15 years, with a minimum amount required each year.

To finish off on the RRSP, I did want to bring up work Group Retirement plans. In many jobs in Canada, the company will match any contribution you make to the Group Retirement Plan. For example, a company may match up to 3% of your contribution, so in such a case, it would make sense to elect to contribute 3% of your salary. By getting the 3% match from your employer, it's an immediate 100% return on investment. The choice of investments will be limited in these Group Retirement plans, since you will only be able to choose from what the Group Retirement fund provider offers. While I believe that TDFs (target-date funds) can be a bit too conservative, however in these Group Retirement plan cases, because of the usually limited options, it may just make sense to go with TDFs as a simple set it and forget it option. Usually when you login to the fund provider's account, you'll have a page with a list of TDFs grouped together. They'll be named with a bunch of words/characters that don't mean much to you, but within each TDFs name will be a number, which is the TDFs retirement year. You should pick the one that corresponds as close to the year that you plan to retire in. For example:

- Manulife Mercer TDF CA 2040: this would correspond to retiring in 2040.
- Manulife Mercer TDF CA 2045: this would correspond to retiring in 2045.
- Manulife Mercer TDF CA 2050: this would correspond to retiring in 2050.

Note that the above are completely made up hypothetical names, just for illustrative examples.

3: FHSA

The FSHA is relatively new, and came out to Canadians in 2023, and is designed for buying your first home. You can open an account when you've turned 18, but will accumulate contribution room only once you open a FHSA account. Contribution room accumulates independent of whether you have previous earned income. When you withdraw to buy your first home, the withdrawal is not taxed. The account can be open for 15 years. Unlike the TFSA however, the contribution room each year is $8,000 annually and not inflation adjusted for the time being, plus up to $8,000 of your unused contribution room from a previous year. For example:

- **2023**: Contributed $1,000 of the $8,000 total available contribution room.
- **2024**: Contribution room is now $15,000 ($7,000 unused amount of 2023 + $8,000 2024 contribution room). In 2024, you again only contribute $1,000
- **2025**: Contribution room is now $16,000 ($8,000 2025 contribution room + $8,000 of the $14,000 unused from 2024. You now have $6,000 unused contribution room from 2024 that you could not use in 2025.
- **2026**: If you used up all of your contribution room of $16,000 in the prior year (2025), then you can then use all of the unused $6,000 in current year (2026). This allows you to use all previously remaining unused contribution room accumulated from 2023 and 2024.

The maximum lifetime limit for the FHSA is $40,000. So if you contribute $8,000 each year, you'd max out by the fifth year, even though you still have 10 years left on the lifespan of the FHSA. Like the RRSP, contributions to the FHSA are tax deductible, however, unlike the RRSP, you do not need to pay back the withdrawal for your home purchase. If you haven't purchased a home after 15 years, the FHSA must be transferred with no tax implications into a RRSP (it is a transfer that will not impact RRSP contribution room). The other scenario for closing a FHSA is if you reached the age of 71, even if the account hasn't been opened for 15 years. In such a scenario, it'll need to be transferred to a RRIF. Like the TFSA and RRSP, over contributions are penalized.

4: TFSA vs. RRSP. vs. FHSA

The TFSA is an extremely powerful tool as I already mentioned, as everything grows tax-free, and isn't taxed upon withdrawal, so it's really flexible. But the RRSP also has advantages, one major one comes from tax deferral and the likelihood that most people in retirement probably will be in a lower tax bracket. These key points, coupled with the fact that most people start their careers off in a lower tax bracket and have higher salaries later in their careers, would mean that it may make more sense at least initially, to favour the TFSA over the RRSP. Especially given the TFSAs flexibility. Unless you are in a career where the starting salary is extremely high and puts you at the highest tax bracket right away for example, then you would need to assess based on your individual circumstances.

For young people that are both early in their careers and looking at buying their home in the next 15 years, the FHSA makes sense, as it essentially takes the strengths from both the TFSA and RRSP. Essentially, it may be ideal, depending on your exact circumstances, for a young person starting out their career, that also has home ownership as a goal within 15 years, to prioritize as such: FHSA > TFSA > RRSP. But again, this really depends on your individual circumstances, and is not a rule.

FHSA, TFSA, and RRSP Summary

	FHSA	TFSA	RRSP
Purpose	First home	Any purpose	Retirement, but can be used for Home Buyers Plan
When contribution room starts	When FHSA account is opened	18 years	When you have earned income
Are contributions tax deductible?	Yes	No	Yes
Are growth/ dividends/ interest tax-sheltered?	Yes	Yes	Yes
Are withdrawals tax free?	Yes (but only for home purchase)	Yes	No
Unused contribution room carries forward?	Yes (but only a max. of $8,000 of previous years unused room)	Yes	Yes

5: RESP

The RESP allows you to contribute and invest for your child's post-secondary education/training. Each year, the government will give you 20% in CESG grants on up to $2,500 of contributions, plus a maximum of one previous years unused contribution room (i.e. for any given year, you can receive the 20% CESG grants on up to $5,000 of contributions).

A "lifetime" total of therefore $36,000 in contributions is required to get the maximum possible CESG grants ($7,200 in total). The last year RESP contributions can be made is in the calendar year of when the child turns 17, and ends on December 31st of the year the child turns 17. Therefore, If starting at year 1 of RESP (child's "age 0"):

- At $2,500/year, you will max out grants by year 15 of the RESP (14 years of age for the child).
- At $2,000/year you will max out grants by year 18 of RESP (17 yrs of age for the child). This is if you want to spread contributions over the entire eligible period.
- The last possible age to start contributing to still get maximum CESG grants, would be at year 11 of the RESP (10 years of age for the child), since the government will only match up to a maximum of $5,000 in contributions each year (only one year can be caught up on in any given year). You therefore need a minimum of 8 years of contribution time to receive maximum grants - an example contribution schedule for such a scenario is shown in the table that follows.

One note is that if a child was born on December 31st, in theory their parents would only have one day to contribute for year 1 of the RESP, which in most cases probably won't be feasible. That's where you would use the CESG grant process of catching up on one previous year's contribution, in any given year.

Second note is that there can also be provincial matching too. For example, Quebec QESI provides an additional 10% on up to a lifetime maximum of $3,600 per child. As of right now, only Quebec and British Columbia offer provincial benefits. It is therefore worth looking into your specific province's RESP guidelines to see at the time when you begin your RESP journey, to see what offerings may be available.

Example Contribution Schedule for Last Possible Year to Start RESP for Maximum CESG

RESP Year	Child's Age	Contribution	CESG Amount
11	10	$4,500	$900
12	11	$4,500	$900
13	12	$4,500	$900
14	13	$4,500	$900
15	14	$4,500	$900
16	15	$4,500	$900
17	16	$4,500	$900
18	17	$4,500	$900
Total		**$36,000**	**$7,200**

Like the other accounts already discussed, the RESP also allows tax-sheltered growth. When the student (your child) is ready to start post-secondary education/training, the funds can be withdrawn, and are taxed at the students income tax bracket (so usually no tax, since many students don't work, or may only work part-time with a low income). If they choose not to pursue post-secondary education/training, then the money can be taken back by you (minus the grants). It can be either withdrawn (the amount due to dividends/interest/growth is taxable to you, but not the original contribution amounts since they were your already-taxed dollars) or transferred without tax-implications into a RRSP up to a maximum government defined limit of currently $50,000 (subject to available RRSP contribution room as well).

In terms of where the RESP lies in the overall priority of all the account types, this is not something I can make suggestions on in this book. Unlike FHSA vs. TFSA vs. RESP where I provided a general guideline that *could* work for most young people that have the goal of home ownership, the RESP is truly “personal finance”. There will be parents that believe investing in their kids takes priority over anything else, including themselves. But then there will be parents that believe they should ensure they have built a solid financial plan for themselves first - the whole “put on your oxygen mask first, before assisting others”. So in this sense, I will leave the decision on RESP priority to the individual reader.

APPENDIX 2
CANADIAN ASSET ALLOCATION FUNDS

I've compiled a list of the asset allocation funds that are popular in Canada, from the major fund providers. This list is definitely not a complete list of all available offerings, especially since more and more fund providers are putting them out. These are just the popular and commonly suggested ones. It's just to serve as a starting point. But in saying that, the funds are generally very similar and globally diversified, with a Canadian home country bias.

In addition, the fund parameters and fees (MER) can change over time. For the most part, due to the increasing competition, the fees have trended down for the funds actually. All the information is provided as is, and reflect the information from the fund providers at the time of writing this book.

The ETFs are extremely popular, but I have also included mutual funds. The reason for including the mutual funds, is that some brokerages will charge a commission fee each time you buy or sell an ETF, but allow you to buy and sell mutual funds commission-free. For example, TD Direct Investing is one such example as of now. Furthermore, Vanguard asset allocation mutual funds are designed to be exactly identical in the underlying holdings to their asset allocation ETFs, so they can be very useful in cases where a brokerage allows commission-free mutual funds trading.

1: ETFs

Vanguard Asset Allocation ETFs

Ticker Symbol	Stocks / bonds (%)	MER (%)
VEQT	100 / 0	0.24
VGRO	80 / 20	0.24
VBAL	60 / 40	0.24
VCNS	40 / 60	0.25
VCIP	20 / 80	0.25

BlackRock Asset Allocation ETFs

Ticker Symbol	Stocks / bonds (%)	MER (%)
XEQT	100 / 0	0.20
XGRO	80 / 20	0.20
XBAL	60 / 40	0.20
XCNS	40 / 60	0.20
XINC	20 / 80	0.20

BMO Asset Allocation ETFs

Ticker Symbol	Stocks / bonds (%)	MER (%)
ZEQT	100 / 0	0.20
ZGRO	80 / 20	0.20
ZBAL	60 / 40	0.20
ZCON	40 / 60	0.20

TD Asset Allocation ETFs

Ticker Symbol	Stocks / bonds (%)	MER (%)
TEQT	100 / 0	0.15^
TGRO	90 / 10	0.17
TBAL	60 / 40	0.17
TCON	30 / 70	0.17
^This is only the partial fee. The fund is new, and the final MER has not yet been calculated.		

2: Mutual Funds

Vanguard Asset Allocation Mutual Funds

Mutual Fund Symbol	Stocks / bonds (%)	MER (%)
VIC1000	100 / 0	0.22^
VIC8020	80 / 20	0.22^
VIC6040	60 / 40	0.22^
VIC4060	40 / 60	0.22^
^This is only the partial fee. The fund is new, and the final MER has not yet been calculated.		

The below summarizes which Vanguard ETF that the mutual funds are meant to mimic:

- VIC1000 mimics VEQT.
- VIC8020 mimics VGRO.
- VIC6040 mimics VBAL.
- VIC4060 mimics VCNS.

TD Asset Allocation Mutual Funds

Mutual Fund Symbol	Stocks / bonds (%)	MER
TDB3179	100 / 0	0.50
TDB3178	80 / 20	0.50
TDB3177	60 / 40	0.50

ABOUT THE PUBLISHER

GANG LAMBIE & SONS

Founded in 2025 by Bevan Gang and Hadlee Lambie, Gang Lambie & Sons is a private family investment firm and publishing company.

We specialize in strategic investments in long-term opportunities, and publish original books and educational resources focused on personal finance, with a mission to educate and empower others on their path to financial freedom.

In addition, we have strong philanthropic visions for the betterment of our local communities. Bevan Gang is passionate about animal welfare, and is a long-time donor to the Montreal SPCA[36]. Gang Lambie & Sons is dedicated to carrying forward any of our families future philanthropic endeavours.

[36] The Montreal SPCA saves hundreds to thousands of abandoned, neglected or mistreated animals each month. SPCA organizations around the world need our support!

TO GET IN TOUCH OR STAY CONNECTED

Visit us at **GangLambieAndSons.com**
For news, updates, blogs and new educational resources.

www.ingramcontent.com/pod-product-compliance
Lightning Source LLC
LaVergne TN
LVHW090419210926
848480LV00002B/623